WHERE TO FROM HERE?

WHERE
TO
FROM
HERE?

WHERE TO FROM HERE?

THE CHRISTIAN VISION OF LIFE AFTER DEATH

BRIAN GROGAN, SJ

New City Press
Hyde Park, New York

To Ethna

Give beauty back, beauty, beauty, beauty, back to God, beauty's self and beauty's giver

Gerard Manley Hopkins

Published in the United States by New City Press
202 Comforter Blvd., Hyde Park, NY 12538
www.newcitypress.com
©2012 Brian Grogan

Cover design by Durva Correia

Library of Congress Cataloging-in-Publication Data:
Grogan, Brian, 1937-
  Where to from here? : the Christian vision of life after death / Brian Grogan.
    p. cm.
  ISBN 978-1-56548-452-8 (pbk. : alk. paper) 1. Future life--Christianity. 2. Heaven--Christianity.
I. Title.
  BT903.G76 2012
  236'.2--dc23

                    2012017605

Printed in the United States of America

Contents

Introduction

Amust-see for tourists in Barcelona is the unfinished cathedral, La Sagrada Familia (The Holy Family), now a UNESCO World Heritage site. Antoni Gaudi began work on it in 1883, but at his death in 1926 less than a quarter of the project was complete — a fact that Gaudi took philosophically when he remarked, "My client is not in a hurry." Other architects have played their part since then, although not without criticism from their colleagues. Mid-point in the construction of this extraordinary work was reached in 2010 and completion is planned perhaps for the centenary of the architect's death.

Attempting a book on the world to come brings elements of Gaudi's project to mind. Firstly, God doesn't seem to be in a hurry or to have a completion date for the epic of world history, but enough of the grand design is available to us to allow some sense of the final masterpiece. Secondly, whereas only approved architects are allowed to leave their mark on the unfinished cathedral in Barcelona, every inhabitant of this planet contributes to the shaping of God's project — the life of the world to come.

This book considers life after death through the lens of relationships. So as you move through it, or if you find yourself puzzled at any point, it will help to remember that key word: "relationships." To a child or an outsider — and to many insiders also — Christian belief can seem like an enormous jumble of disconnected facts, but each aspect of faith is to be understood in terms of the divine-human relationships established among us by Jesus. Thus, while we are surrounded by mystery, the concept of relationships offers a dynamic and unchanging viewpoint which illuminates every aspect of the world to come.

Pastoral Context

Although mortality is an unavoidable fact, theological study of the afterlife is still fairly uncommon in Christian circles. Of greater popular interest is the experiential aspect of relationships with those who have died. Some people attest to being aware of the death of a loved one before being told, and many of us have a sense of connectedness with someone who has died. All Souls' Day, with prayers and the blessing of graves, is a major pastoral event. The month of November brings crowds to Catholic churches to remember their departed ones in rite and symbol and in the Altar List of the Dead. Funerals, especially of younger people, can remind pastors of the past when churches were better attended. Remembrances of the dead are a healthy reaction to death, because we are spirit-enfleshed, and we want to keep bonded with those relatives and friends with whom we have shared so much of life, with its joy and tears.

This strong belief in the continued life of "the dead" sets the pastoral context for the explorations herein. I hope to provide a theological background to the Christian practice of remembering those who have gone before us, and to indicate what we can say in faith about how things are with them now. This book may encourage conversation about topics of ultimate importance, which otherwise are left unspoken. This often happens when someone is terminally ill and everyone knows but nothing is said, because no one knows what to say.

Limits of this Book

To establish the scope of this book, some clarifications are in order. Firstly, while the writings of saints, mystics and poets can provide valuable insights into what the future may hold for us, this work is based in the Christian scriptures and Christian theology. Secondly, I will not be dealing with Near-Death Experiences (NDEs), except to say that the reader will note points of convergence between many of these reports and the theological findings. Scientific research is understandably critical of the claim that NDEs give us insights into what awaits us after death. But we are here on the point of intersection of two worlds — the human and the divine — and along this border, science and religion must negotiate with mutual respect and caution. Thirdly, although not a topic in this book, the issue of communication with those who have died is to be taken seriously. "There are more things in heaven and earth than are dreamt of in your philosophy" as Hamlet remarks, and there are indeed grounds for asserting that there can exist communication between living and dead, of a sensitive if not a dramatic kind. C. S. Lewis has expressed what went on in him, unbidden and unexpected, after the death of his beloved wife, Joy. This has awakened some of his readers — and I include myself here — to a sensitivity towards the unobtrusive but solid presence of a deceased beloved: "The sound of a chuckle in the darkness ... so business-like ... yet there was a cheerful intimacy ... Solid. Utterly reliable. Firm. There is no nonsense about the dead..."[1]

G. W. Hughes SJ, author of the bestselling *God of Surprises*, touches on his sense of the presence of his sisters who had died tragically. They were, he remarks, like shy guests at a cocktail party who turned out to be the best of company once you gently engaged with them:

> In imagination, I speak to Marie, and to the rest of my family, who are now all dead. Margot, like Marie, is close to me, a strengthening, reassuring presence ... Somehow their good and my good are identical.[2]

Irish TV broadcaster John Quinn wrote to his wife, Olive, after her death:

> I believe in your presence totally. That's why I talk to you all the time. You are in the light. It's me that needs the letters ... I am at once heartbroken by your absence and consumed by your "presence" — more in love with you than I ever thought possible ... I know you give me little signs now and then, and I know I must be patient.[3]

Such intimate revelations are congruent with what many people experience. We differ in our levels of awareness of reality, and those with exceptional awareness can challenge us to tune into a new frequency. As we shall see below, human solidarity and the communion of saints offers a theological underpinning, in terms of relationships, of our widespread experience of connectedness with those for whom we cared.

---

1. C. S. Lewis, *A Grief Observed* (London: Faber & Faber, 1961), pp. 60–1.
2. G.W. Hughes SJ, *God, Where Are You?* (London: DLT, 1997), p. 55, p. 85.
3. John Quinn, *Letters to Olive: Sea of Love, Sea of Loss, Seed of Love, Seed of Life* (Dublin: Veritas, 2011), p. 129.

Terminology

Finding a suitable title for this book was difficult, because there is
no satisfactory term to name what none of us have yet experienced.
"The life of the world to come" expresses the Creeds, but it suggests
a radical discontinuity from this life, as does the term "afterlife."
"Human fulfillment" catches the continuity between the next life
and the present, but can seem too psychological and personalist.
"Graced fulfillment" catches the Christian dimension. "End" is a
bit stark, though one of my professors liked it. "Eschatology" and
"*eschaton*" (from the Greek, meaning "end") are forbidding terms.
The traditional term "The Four Last Things" lacks dynamism and
ignores the relevance of the future to the present. "The Lasting
Things" better connects the two.

The title finally chosen reflects the radical question hidden in
our hearts: "Where to from here?" The subtitle acknowledges that
the book offers a Christian response to that issue. In a world beset
by confusion, anxiety and meaninglessness, Christianity offers a
grounded and hopeful vision of the future of humankind which
merits serious attention.

Again, how should we refer to those who have died? Are they to
be called "the dead"? Hardly, since Jesus asserts that to God everyone
is alive (cf. Mk 12:27, Mt 22:32). For Christians, then, there are no
"dead" but only those who "have died." The term "faithful departed"
acknowledges the reality of death, but have the dead indeed departed,
or does that spatial metaphor do a disservice to the reality? In these
pages a variety of terms will be used, though each is inadequate to
convey the full reality of what is yet to come.

Format

Some readers may be disconcerted by the fact that there is too long
a run-in to the discussion of the world to come. "Why not cut to the
chase?" they say, "this would make the book shorter and more direct."
But these are uncertain times for belief, hence a solid groundwork
will help some readers. Also, we will be dealing with the evolving
present rather than jumping straight into the future. While there is

discontinuity between this world and the next, there is also continuity — life is changed, not ended. So only if we grasp the lasting things as given to us now will we be able to project forward rightly. Gaudi's successors can move his unfinished cathedral toward completion only when they contemplate the existing construction, immerse themselves in his vision, and study his remaining sketches. Likewise here: present and future reality must interplay and illuminate one another if the final result is to be a masterpiece.

Each topic will begin and end with questions, to assist personal appropriation of the issue under consideration. Questions, when answered, lead to further wondering, so suggestions for additional reading are sprinkled through the text. Since the divine is characterized by intelligent imagination, readings around the future which God dreams for us should stimulate in turn both the left and right brain. Imagination is strongly linked to good theology.[4] Hence I have found C. S. Lewis' writings very helpful in preparing this book. His *Chronicles of Narnia* are not intended simply to amuse children: they are eschatological in intent. The children are making for a mysterious country in which they will participate in the divine and enjoy an intimate relationship with the Creator. This is what eschatology is all about!

---

4. To explore this link you might read J. T. Sellars, *Reasoning Beyond Reasoning: Imagination as a Theological Source in the Work of C. S. Lewis* (Oregon: Pickwick Publications, 2011).

- PART ONE -

Starting Points

Why Believe in God?

Does God Exist?

*B*elief in a worthwhile afterlife depends on accepting the existence of God. But does God exist? Perhaps you have no difficulty with this question, and if that be so, it is a blessing: you are in tune with people of countless ages who have taken the existence of God for granted. But for the sake of readers who, like myself, often have to renew their decision to believe in God in the light of human evil and natural disasters, I will outline my personal reasons for believing.

Let's admit that God doesn't make things easy for believers! What do you say when asked: "If God exists and sustains us, why the misery of millions on the planet today?" "Why doesn't God simply destroy the wicked?" "Why is God so hidden? A big revelation would answer our doubts." "Why do bad things happen to good people and why does God allow tsunamis and other disasters?" I have no intention here of addressing the issue of God's existence in a way that would satisfy a scientifically-minded sceptic. The existence of God cannot be proved or disproved by scientific criteria. Theists believe God exists; atheists believe there is no God. Reasonable evidence for either position can be adduced. Scientists, atheists, humanists and believers share a common love for "our garden planet." My simple purpose here is to outline elements of my personal *credo*.

The Ultimate "Why?"

We are born with a curiosity which expresses itself in asking the question "Why?" There is in us a desire to know, which drives beyond partial answers to ever further questions. So it appears to me to be fair to ask, "Why does this world exist?" Reality indeed exists all around me, but how can it do so? I came into existence a number of years ago, and at some stage — not too far distant — I will cease to be. So how do I exist at all? "What explains *me*?" is the real issue, rather than "What explains *God*"? For me the existence of material reality needs an explanation, so I judge it reasonable to postulate a Being That Simply Is, the ultimate and necessary cause of all that exists. The world outside my window raises the God-issue for me. Where did it come from and what keeps it in existence? As an amateur gardener I find nature mysterious, wonderful, fascinating. Behind it and within it I believe there must be a Being who is even more mysterious, wonderful and fascinating.

The scientific mind can explain much about material reality. But the ultimate "Why?" goes beyond the physical, and since science is not the only form of knowledge, to me it is reasonable to go beyond it and to ask the ultimate "Why?" which brings us to what we mean by "God" — the ultimate cause of everything. Like scientists, I believe in an intelligible world, but intelligibility emerges from intelligence. The universe has at least a temporal purpose, and purpose emerges from decision. This indicates to me the *personal* nature of the Being That Simply Is: persons have minds and wills.

Elizabeth Johnson suggests that originally the word "God" may have meant "to take care of and cherish all things, burning all malice like a consuming fire."[1] "Caring and cherishing" expresses the kind of God I believe in. I join in with those who reject a being that would diminish whatever is good about human life, especially freedom and happiness. My concept is of a God who is neither distant nor intrusive, but who enables the fulfillment of the deepest needs and desires implanted in us.

Invisible Yet Real

There exists around us a huge set of invisible yet operative realities. You can't see air, electricity, gravity, radio signals, or nuclear energy, but they're real: put your hand on a live wire and you'll know electricity exists, look at the mushroom cloud over Hiroshima in 1945 and you'll know the awesome power of atomic energy. Likewise, the being I name as "God" can be massively present and active, without being visible. But while these invisible realities can be measured and controlled, God cannot be — despite our best efforts at divine domestication. God is abundantly free.

---

1. Elizabeth Johnson, *She Who Is: The Mystery of God in Feminist Theological Discourse* (New York: Crossroad, 1995), p. 44.

Moving along, there's a lot more to human life than can be observed, measured, compared and controlled. These dimensions include the reality of friendship and love; appreciation of music, art, and literature; prayer, longing, self-sacrifice, forgiveness, religious experience. Such dimensions express the best of us, they sustain us, and their existence is not to be denied simply because it can't be "proved" in lab tests. I can't accept the following comment: "Relationships? They're only fresh air between two persons — and some dust!" Love *exists*: though you can't see it, you know when it is present or absent. You can't tie a relationship down and examine it scientifically, but it is real: a happy couple will tell you it's the most important thing in their lives. We live within a network of relationships, invisible though they may be, and I hold that the primary relationship that sustains us is God's relationship with us.

Reasonable Belief

Every relationship is sustained by belief. People don't know that their partners love them simply by looking at them — instead they *believe* they do. And such belief is not necessarily naïve and groundless. We live our lives by exercising *reasonable* belief. We check for evidence before saying "I think this milk is sour" or "I believe she loves me" or "Chemo is tough, but it will cure my cancer." We decide to believe only when the reasons add up for us. We are faced with an unknown future, but we check the evidence and the reasons before we step into that future. Good decisions emerge from reasonable belief. It is *unfounded* belief that is naïve and leads to bad decisions.

Belief is an essential component of human living, as Lonergan argues in *Insight*.[2] Personally acquired knowledge, he notes, is a rare commodity. In other words, few of us *know* that Ireland is an island; we believe it is. We trust the stock market report or we don't, for reasons that we believe to be sound. Non-scientists and scientists hear of new discoveries, but both groups can only believe them to be true, pending corroboration. Our human world is built on reasonable belief. Successive generations of scientists don't start from ground zero and reinvent the wheel — they take past achievements

---

2.   Bernard Lonergan, *Insight* (London: Longmans, 1957), pp. 703–18.

as starting points for their own work. If flaws emerge, they revisit earlier insights to detect error and then move forward again.

Our lives are sustained by belief. Imagine a world devoid of belief and of its partner, trust. Getting out of bed and having breakfast would be impossible — the floor might give way, the cereal might be poisoned. Human living as we know it would fall apart. Against this scenario the *necessity of reasonable belief* emerges, and belief in God as the answer to the ultimate "Why?" appears less than outlandish in an intelligible world. In fact, to many people, belief in God appears more reasonable than not believing.

Knowledge Born of Love

The above is a labored account of my reasons for believing in God. But of course the living history of my belief began elsewhere: in family love, in a believing environment, in catechesis and education, and in personal experience. William James's *The Varieties of Religious Experience*, and the ensuing multitude of books on the topic, find an echo in the experiences of many people, including the young, who often seem to have an innate religious sense.[3] My religious experiences were helped by time spent in two churches, one awesome and the other intimate. There grew spontaneously a relationship with "God" — whatever God was. Commitment to this relationship through prayer and worship made life comforting and meaningful. While the images of God presented to me were sometimes distorted, they were healthy enough for my personal or inner life to grow, although not of course without ups and downs and blank patches. Just as my parents were present to me long before I reached the use of reason, God was too. I didn't hold off from relating to them until I had decided, "My parents exist!" They were simply there, sustaining and affecting me in each detail of my existence. Likewise, the "Mystery that is fascinating and awesome," Rudolf Otto's phrase for God, was all around. Like everyone else, I was immersed in mystery from the beginning.

We know the experience of finding ourselves in love and how, as the relationship grows, more is revealed: there is a knowledge born

---

3. William James, *The Varieties of Religious Experience* (New York: Touchstone, 1997).

of love. My relationship with God, happily, has kept developing. The Latin word *credo* comes from two smaller words, *cor do*: "I give my heart." To some degree at least I have given my heart to God. This otherwise risky action is sustained by my ongoing experience of God's loving kindness. Let me admit it: I *expect* God to back me up, support me, and enable me to do what I should! Left to myself I would fail, fall apart and cease to exist. I am a cry for help and God meets my needs. I "know" God is around! Good things happen to me, doors open up, insights occur — someone's watching out for me, I am cared about and I know it.

The Good News keeps me going, though it is an unending challenge to believe that God walked this world in human form and died as Jesus died. While God's providence becomes more mysterious, the Christian vision of life makes sense to me. I am helped by the concreteness of the Gospels, while the spirituality that nourishes me challenges me to find God in all things. I am fascinated by the mystery of why people love one another at all, yet love is the fabric which holds society together. Why are most people basically good and why do they devote themselves to the selfless care of others? How did the universe "know that we were coming" and why is there a providence supporting and guiding us? Why is there a yearning in us for "something more" — why don't we simply chew the cud as cows do? The answers to these and other musings cluster for me around a "God" who is relational and caring.

At the same time I labor over my belief, it gets challenged by every TV news program I watch. How can God's goodness be compatible with the suffering and tragedies that humankind endures? Why is God silent? Where the hell is God?[4] Such questions cannot be fully answered in this life. I have to remind myself over and over of the Christian tradition that it is from God that everything good comes and that evil comes from our unreasonable decisions.

---

4. Richard Leonard's *Where the Hell is God?* (New Jersey: Paulist Press, 2010), has been described as a life-changing book, one of the best available on the question of suffering.

Science and Religion

One of my brethren who was quite conservative read the *Tablet* weekly. When asked why, he'd respond: "I want to know what the enemy is thinking!" It may help in ending this chapter to sketch the positions which scientists take up in regard to the God-issue, not to understand an enemy but to be respectfully aware that intelligent people see the same reality differently. Some scientists and believers accept the complementarity of science and theology.[5] *Science and Spirituality: Making Room for Faith in the Age of Science* is written by a convinced atheist, Michael Ruse, who is aware that something important hinges on the question of God's existence.[6] For him, belief in God is *rationally valid*. Science is not the only fruit of human reasoning. On the other hand, religion must not try to explain everything.

Some scientists hold that the universe is self-generating — that it evolves randomly, on its own, without purpose. God, they say, does not exist because God cannot be known through scientific method, which is, for them, the only true way to knowledge. For others, the exploration of cosmic and quantum reality bring a sense of mystery. But, they hold, the universe itself is ultimate: there is no further mystery lurking behind it. Our mysterious world is simply there.

Others again hold for Intelligent Design. Life, they argue, is no random accident. Against all the odds, the universe was so arranged that the emergence of life became a high probability. Thus, they postulate the existence of a being that is intelligence itself, and name it "God." Against this position are scientists who say that evolution itself will explain what has happened, and that the "God of the Gaps" is dragged in only when needed to comfort believers.

At the high end of the belief scale are Creationists. For them, Genesis is to be taken literally. Thus they deny the theory of evolu-

---

5. For a wide-ranging recent account of human origins in the light of creation and evolution, see Brendan Purcell, *From Big Bang to Big Mystery: Human Origins in the Light of Creation and Evolution* (Hyde Park, NY: New City Press, 2012). Writing from a Christian perspective, the author assumes the complementarity of science, philosophy and religion.

6. Michael Ruse, *Science and Spirituality: Making Room for Faith in the Age of Science* (Cambridge: Cambridge University Press, 2010).

tion, especially as it purports to explain the origins of human life. They see science as a threat to faith, and choose the latter.

Among Christian thinkers, Thomas Berry, author with Brian Swimme of *The Universe Story*, defends the divine or the sacred in nature. Appreciation of and respect for the earth, he argues, can be diluted by over-emphasizing a transcendent God: cosmic wonder must be restored lest we destroy the biosphere. A new paradigm is needed if we are rightly to relate faith and science, religion and material reality.

Finally, some Christians believe that religion and science are complementary. All scientific knowledge, they say, including evolution rightly understood, is to be accepted: God is revealed within nature. But, they continue, a dimension of human reality beyond the material and the scientific must be acknowledged. For Christians, the universe story and the Judeo-Christian story are mutually enriching. The latter is to be seen in terms of personal self-communication by the Author of the material universe.[7]

For myself, belief in God seems reasonable on the grounds I have outlined above. As to how the universe came into being, I accept provisionally the current scientific hypothesis, the Big Bang theory — though this is being challenged, at least in some of its details, as in a recent issue of *Scientific American*. But my belief in God does not hang on a scientific hypothesis. I find it reasonable to believe that God has a meaningful project for the world, and that God has communicated something of it to us through what we term "revelation." This leads into the issue of belief in a world to come, which we will address in the following chapter.

---

7.   For further reading in this area, consult Mary Ellen Sheehan, *Four Stories: Integrating the Universe Story, the Christian Story, the Earth Story and the IHM Story* (Monroe, Michigan: IHM Publications, 2007). Karen Armstrong, *The Case for God: What Religion Really Means* (London: Bodley Head, 2009) is also helpful. Noting that for the first time in history, many millions of people want nothing to do with God, she asks why has God become incredible, and she draws on the insights of our predecessors to outline a faith that can speak to our polarized world.

Summary

1. Believing is natural to us. What matters is that it be reasonable.

2. Many people find the reality of suffering and evil incompatible with belief in God.

3. Christians say that belief in God is reasonable, because the universe cannot explain itself.

4. To accommodate the reality of suffering, believers have to abandon the image of a "nice" God in favor of a God who is infinitely mysterious.

For Pondering

◊ If you believe in God, how do you deal with the challenges that suffering and evil present?

◊ If you are a searcher or an agnostic, what do you make of the above argument for belief in God?

Why Believe in an After Life?

To focus our minds on the issue raised in this chapter, let us consider the following comments:

> Last year, my father-in-law died. When I sat at his deathbed, and looked at the body from which life had ebbed, I couldn't help marveling at the persistence of the concept of the afterlife. There he lay, in his frailty and banality, his body the register, the lined book, of his seventy-nine years. The corpse was so palpable in its morbidity, so finished. But for centuries, people believed the book would be opened again.[8]

> Well, could it end with a hole in the ground? ... But I think if you can accept the existence of God, then all the other things are possible. Believing in God and the afterlife is the only way I can make sense of life. It's a huge leap ... Of course, for most of us the unanswerable question is whether or not there is a God and a life after death. There are those who have absolute certainty about eternal life and those who are adamant that eternal life is all "pie in the sky." Those of us in between muddle about, flip-flopping, doubting, hoping and maybe even believing that there is a God out there with whom we will one day share eternal life. I have no trouble saying it's to that category of people I belong. I can also say, with a certain strength and even conviction, that I believe.[9]

The Struggle to Believe

In the previous chapter, I outlined why I find it reasonable to believe in the existence of God. But what of the next step — that is, belief that there is a world to come when earthly life ends? The issue of an afterlife can be a lifelong puzzle, or may come into focus only after losing someone we love, or being faced with a radical lack of meaning in life, as in the black comedy film *The War of the Roses* (1989), in which life falls apart for the couple when the house is perfectly finished. Then new questions arise: Does love die? Does death end everything?

---

8. James Wood, reviewing John Casey, *After Lives: A Guide to Heaven, Hell and Purgatory* (Oxford: Oxford University Press, 2010) in *London Review of Books*, vol. 33 no. 8, 14 April 2011.

9. Bishop Willie Walsh, *Irish Times*, 6 November 2010.

Will I ever be reunited with the person who meant everything to me? And even if there is an afterlife, do friendships endure there?

Tell Me Your Name!

I have said that the visible world, in all its wonder and complexity, makes me ask what sort of Being keeps it going. From the time the human race first emerged — about 150,000 years ago — people have speculated about the ultimate "Why?" of things. Hence the phenomenon of world religions and their varied concepts of God. That this Being must be personal seems obvious. An impersonal force won't do: this Being must have, in some super-eminent way, the qualities that "It" shares with us — understanding and love and all else.

Granting the existence of this personal Being, the possibility of its self-revelation seems appropriate. That God might reveal the divine name strikes me as delightful. It opens up the possibility of friendship. You can hardly have a friendship with someone who withholds their name! Yet the name given in the Hebrew account — "I AM WHO I AM" (Ex 3:14) — is full of mystery. It must certainly mean "I just am!" but much more too. It distinguishes God from all other beings. We humans cannot say, "We just are!" because our existence is contingent on the couple who became our parents, just as their existence depended on their parents. But God has no ancestry: God has been there all the time, is just so, and always will be. That this self-revelation of God was given historically first to a tiny group in a remote place rather than to everyone at once, respects how discoveries unfold and spread out slowly across space and time.

Revelation

That God should talk to human beings does not seem inappropriate to me: parents talk to their infants long before the latter can respond, and children grow by reaching up to the minds of their parents. If God has plans and dreams for us, he needs to share them with us so that we can direct our lives by them. So we are told through Genesis that from the beginning of our existence we are in relationship with a communicating God. The *Dictionary of Biblical Theology* notes that the Hebrew mind thought it nonsense to speak of human beings outside their relationship with God, whereas to many today the notion of "divine revelation" seems like an interruption, an interference, a threat to our freedom and our independence. To the Hebrews it was otherwise: God reveals that his heart is set on them, that he will direct and guide them, provide for them and keep them safe. This gives that tiny band of nomads a unique meaning, and they know it. God establishes an open relationship of love with the "Chosen People" and biblical history chronicles the troubled and unequal relationship between the Jews and their God.

The Human Face of God

That God's engagement should move from speech to personal presence among us is to me an unpredictable but wonderful surprise. Divine self-revelation reaches its high point here. God decides to become human, with all the vulnerability and limitation that this involves. The incarnation makes God accessible. We can look at the man, Jesus, see how he goes about things, and realize that this is what God is like and what God thinks about us. Hence the unending scope for contemplation of what Jesus said and did, and why he suffered, died and rose again. The evidence for Jesus' resurrection from death is sufficient for me to believe that he is the Son of God. No other explanation, I feel, will do. But I can understand why others don't find the evidence compelling and I quietly marvel that it is agreeable to God to leave us to speculate endlessly regarding Jesus' claims.

Promise of Eternal Life

The "Good News" that Jesus preaches is that God is in love with us and wants to engage us in eternal friendship. Why God should do this is a mystery to me, but love is free and needs no prior explanation for its choice. It is this desire of God that provides the context for my belief in an afterlife: but an afterlife of a glorious kind. "Hades" and "Sheol" conjured up for the Hebrews banishment from the world of God and endless wandering in darkness, because one cannot die and be done with existence. Instead, the words of Jesus are full of promise, and promises are the language of love. He offers a fulfillment that exceeds our wildest hopes and dreams by inviting us into the very life of God. The friendship begun when Jesus first reached out his hand to Simon Peter is to endure beyond death. "You will sit at my table in my kingdom" (Lk 22:28-30). The disciples are promised a hundredfold in this age, and in the age to come, eternal life (Mk 10:30). Peter could not prove that these promises would be fulfilled. But he knew enough of Jesus to believe them.

Like Peter, I have to renew my decision to believe what I cannot prove. I find it fitting that God should intend a resolution of human life that would make ultimate sense of it. Nothing less would make up for the chaos of human history, where many people never get a chance and most people suffer a great deal.

Jesus' promise is that we will be where he is, and that "our joy will never be taken away" (Jn 14:3; 16:20). Of course, I'd like more evidence to back up this divine promise: it would help so much if those who have died could come back, even once, to tell us that it's all true. But I have to make do with what is given — the resurrection of Jesus and the promise that he will take us to where he is. I have to decide over and over again to cling to a belief that God, as Einstein said, is mysterious but not malicious. I have to battle with the negative indicators suggested by genocides and tsunamis. "Does God exist'?" I say "Yes." "Do suffering and evil also exist?" "Yes." These truths are not incompatible if it can be shown that God works within evil and suffering to bring good out of them. The lesson of the Passion is that this is precisely God's way of acting, as in the title of a book by Balthasar: *Love Alone: The Way of Revelation* (1968). What was the worst of Fridays becomes *Good* Friday only because of the love involved: it cuts across the downward spiral of evil, sin and death and it opens up to humankind a new world of freedom and love, God's world.

Laughter at the End

A physicist, who once gave me the "Ladybird" version of electrons, said that reality as we know it is marvelously interconnected. Electrons at either end of the universe vibrate in synchronicity with one another. "So true is this," he said, "that we can't understand anything by itself, but only in its connectedness. Everyone is linked with everyone else — past, present and future. Which means that only when the last of the human race has been gathered in will we know the full story. So history is like a cosmic joke. While you're telling a joke, people are puzzled. They wonder how the story is going to work out. Only with the punch line do they get the point and laugh." So it is with the human story: I must be patient. Only at the end will the point be clear. Then the laughter will begin, laughter of the purest and most liberating kind, a laughter led by the three divine Persons who always intended that things would end well and who labored mightily to bring this about.

Summary

1. The goodness of the material world and of human beings grounds belief that its originator is good and wishes us well.
2. That this Being might help us by self-revelation is not unreasonable.
3. Jesus, the self-revelation of God, sees what we are like but also what we can become. He has hope for humankind and promises us eternal friendship.
4. Suffering is to be explained not by denying the existence of a good God but by observing how God brings good out of evil.

For Pondering

◊ What instances can you find in which good emerges out of evil? Could this be an indicator for you that God is at work?

Why Write About Life After Death?

A Doubtful Future?

"*Y*ou all want to go to heaven, isn't that true?" said the preacher. "Yes!" responded the congregation enthusiastically. "Well, raise your right hand if you want to go there now!" Silence: heads down. Eventually a few hands went up, the hands of those who felt that, upon mature reflection, they had had enough of this life. If you had been there, would you have raised your hand? Or if you were asked to talk on TV for five minutes about what you expect after death, would you be able to fill the time? My own interest in matters eschatological began over forty years ago, and what was then an academic concern has developed a certain urgency with the passing of years! But what precisely is eschatology?

Eschatology and Freedom

We noted earlier that the Greek word *eschaton* (plural: *eschata*) means an ultimate, final, last thing. So eschatology refers to that branch of theology which deals with the culmination of the history of humankind. It has its center in the gracious decision of God to bring both humankind and the material world into divine life. We are not asking the scientific question: What will happen as the life of planet Earth comes to an end? We ask instead the radical question: what are God's intentions for us and for our world?

The evidence for Christian eschatology comes from divine revelation. Eschatology, as we shall see, forms a single symphony with all of Christian theology. We mentioned earlier Purcell's *From Big Bang to Big Mystery*. "Big Bang" refers to the origins of the cosmos, and "Big Mystery" to the origin of human beings. Eschatology completes that sweep by dealing with the world to come, so this book might have been called *From Big Bang through Big Mystery to Final Resolution*.

What is God planning as our final destiny? If asked to choose between God having a blueprint or a game plan, which would you choose? I choose the latter, because what God is about is not our submission but our freedom, a gift we value so much. God is free and invites us to be free also. Parents, at their best, want their children to mature into fully free persons; likewise God desires this for us. Freedom is not simply the capacity to do nothing or to be selfish, but to express our human potential fully and appropriately. And freedom is the gift that Jesus brings. The New Testament is full of it: this is why it is called Good News. Jesus proclaims freedom for captives and the oppressed (cf. Lk 4:18). His divine task was to eliminate all forms of domination.[10] Paul asserts: "For freedom Christ has set us free!" (Gal 5:1). The whole story of salvation is linked with liberation from the traps of political slavery, sin, law and death that inhibit God's people from living life to the full in loving friendship with God and one another. "Where the Spirit of the Lord is, there is freedom" (2 Cor 3:17). Balthasar goes so far as to say that perfect freedom is our eschatological goal, and that the call of God, "Be holy as I am holy" (1 Pt 1:16), means "Be free as I am free."[11] This can help to dispel our fear that God is out to limit our autonomy. God is not a dominating God, but instead wants to make us "fully alive," as St. Irenaeus said long ago. That is the game plan.

Eschatology in Eclipse

Although it should be the most exciting branch of Christian thought, eschatology receives scant treatment nowadays. Several reasons can be given for its eclipse.

1. Negative Connotation

A bed-ridden colleague who felt I was taking eschatology too seriously said to me one day: "Young man, I'll tell you about the Four Last Things. First there's the room, when you can't get out except in

---

10. Walter Wink's *Engaging the Powers: Discernment and Resistance in a World of Domination* (Minnesota: Fortress Press, 1992), shows how Jesus undercuts all forms of domination — against women, children, religious and social outcasts. Sickness, sin, demonic possession and even death are Jesus' targets too, hence the cures, exorcisms, resuscitations and forgiveness of sins. The goal of the kingdom of heaven is to make everyone free to be their freest and best selves. We have our role to play in the elimination of domination.

11. See *The von Balthasar Reader*, ed. M. Kehl & W. Loser (Edinburgh: T&T Clark, 1982), p. 108.

a wheelchair. Then there's your chair — you get stuck in that. Next last thing is the bed, which I'm confined in now. And last there'll be the box, when you're nailed in! There are your Four Last Things, so forget all this new theology!" So much for enlightened curiosity regarding the final state of humankind! Poor catechesis led many good people to a benumbing fear of death and a judgment darkened by the possibility of final loss. So they shied away from the issue, reasoning, "If we don't think about it, it will go away!" I hope these pages will help to reverse that trend and lead to healthy discussion about what lies ahead.

2. Vatican II

Surprisingly, Vatican II (1962–65) didn't help the cause of eschatology. Until the sixties, the Church was strongly focused on the world to come, so much so that in the popular mind the goal of Christian living was to squeeze through the pearly gates, even if it took a deathbed conversion to get you over the line! The shaping of this world in preparation for the eschaton was largely ignored, as were ecological concerns, since it was taken for granted that matter would be superfluous in the final scheme of things. With Vatican II however, the Church rightly began to take seriously its task of transforming contemporary society in the light of the Gospel. And since it is hard to focus on two huge realities at the one time, the here-and-now struggle for justice and liberation prevailed over concerns about the world to come. Hence the joke in theological circles that "eschatology is closed for repairs!"

3. Decline in Christian Belief

The general decline in Christian belief has many causes which lie outside the scope of the present pages. But the consequence is that ours is an impoverished climate for discussing the afterlife. Many of my one-time fellow Catholics are now, understandably, alienated from the Church and seriously critical of its teachings. Some of my own family are humanists. Where previously the convictions of others buoyed up the Christian community, now those convictions are often dormant, if not erased. The dominance of scientific thinking plays its part in the decline of belief. Thus Richard Dawkins and others claim to have discredited the notion of God, and some neuroscientists assert that they have found the "god part" of the brain, a mental department which invents and deals with "god issues." Believers are hard pressed by such claims, and older explanations of Christian eschatological belief have withered in the face of intelligent criticism.

We live in a time of confusion on many levels. The old has run out, the new is not yet in sight. The postmodern way is to take a skeptical approach to long-range issues. Scholars like Bernard Lonergan support Karl Jasper's contention that we are living in an axial phase of human history; that is, all is currently being reconfigured. Thus, with old certainties discredited, comments on the life of the world to come are greeted with incredulity or apathy.

Hence, while the fact of death surrounds us and I attend far more funerals than I care to think of, denial of death is the fashion of our times. "Heaven" is now the name of a tanning shop in Dublin, "Heavenly Manna" is a deli! "Mission Eternity" means that we will live forever in all our details, but on a database. "Ecstasy" is a drug, not an experience of closeness to God. Ageing is simply an illness which will soon be curable. Life expectancy will run to one hundred and fifty years — which recalls the dialogue between a smoker and his daughter: "But Daddy, people who don't smoke live longer!" "Serves them right!" he said. Belief however still lingers, even if it often has little underpinning. At a recent solemn funeral which I attended in Coventry Cathedral, the voice of Vera Lynn rang out as the coffin was wheeled up the church: "We'll meet again, don't know where, don't know when …" If Vera Lynn managed to console the British troops in World War II with at least a dim hope that not everything ends with death, have we today any intelligent hope to offer the dying and those who grieve for them?

4. Deafening Silence

My long-suffering mother was a sounding board for my raw ideas and uncritical enthusiasm regarding matters eschatological. When I'd ask, "What do you think?" she would say, "That's all fine in theory, Brian, but how do we know there's anything there? If only someone came back to tell." I'd leap in to remind her of Jesus returning to instruct his disciples after the resurrection, but while she'd nod, she would add, "Well, I don't know. No one *else* ever came back." She had a point, and I understand why friends — and I include good Christians — roll their eyes when I say I'm trying to write about the world to come. A first reaction is, "Why bother?" The polite "How very interesting!" means, "Oh my God, let's talk about something else." An honest comment is, "Haven't we trouble enough trying to understand this world without trying to crack the code of the next one?" But then there's a small group who say, "Oh my, tell me where you've got to!" which means that they've questions about the future in their own hearts.

"Is death the end of everything?" That question has been raised since the beginning of human life on earth, once our first ancestors began to ponder on what had become of one of their number who had died. When at some stage, perhaps 150,000 years ago, our early ancestors became reflective, death became a mystery. I can imagine a Neanderthal coming home from the hunt to find his partner prone and lifeless. Perhaps he sat down and wondered what had happened. "What is missing that was present when I went out?" How long a period elapsed before our ancestors thought about the "spirit" of a person? Then the questions: "Where does the spirit go? Does it live on in some better place? Perhaps death is not the end for us?" We search then, alongside that endless line of people over 150 millennia who have looked at the mystery of death and tried to see what it can mean.

"Where To From Here?"

The question "Where to from here?" won't go away, even though, as after the carnage of 9/11, it is rarely asked in public. This despite the fact that the deaths on that awful day were the most publicized in all of human history. While Christianity offers dramatic insights to this question and opens out a vast vision of the life to come, operative theology lags behind. Many believers adopt a "wait and see" attitude. Some believe in God, but not in a life to come; others believe in an afterlife, but not in God! For one parent I know, the issue of the afterlife first arose only when her child asked as a funeral was passing, "Mom, what's in that nice brown box with the flowers on it?" Then, "Mom, will you die too?" And then, "Where will you go? Can I come too?"

You don't have to be a practicing Christian to be saved or to enter the next life, but if you are a Christian, certain things follow. Christianity is *massively future-oriented.* It claims that through the intervention of God in Jesus Christ, our lives now not only have present but ultimate meaning; that our destiny lies beyond this present world; that we are in fact made to be with God eternally. To truly be a Christian is to commit oneself to belief in the life of the world to come. It is to see eternal life as our inheritance, held in trust for us by a loving God.

The Old Testament and the New differ like night and day in their focus on the life to come. There is only a trickle of texts from the Hebrew Bible (the Old Testament) expressing hope in life beyond death. In Jesus' day, the Pharisees believed in life after death, while the Sadducees did not. Before he met Jesus, Peter the fisherman might have had a vague expectation of a worthwhile life to come, but he had no evidence to support his hope.

Christ is Risen!

This caution and ambivalence about eternal life with God are swept away by a torrent of conviction when we move from the Hebrew to the Christian scriptures. The alleged fact of the resurrection of Jesus Christ is its guarantee. Jesus' statement to Martha after the death of her brother summarizes New Testament belief: *"I am the resurrection and the life.* Those who believe in me, even though they die, will live, and everyone who lives and believes in me *will never die"* (Jn 11:25-26).

Christian worship echoes this theme of eternal life. The Eucharist, which sums up Christian belief, begins by asking God to forgive our sins and to bring us to *everlasting life.* The Creed proclaims our belief in *the resurrection of the dead, and the life of the world to come.* In the offertory we ask that we may come to *share in the divinity of Christ.* In the Eucharistic prayers we ask God that we may share *eternal life* with Mary and the saints, and we pray that the Holy Spirit may make us *an everlasting gift* to God. Communion is seen as a participation in *eternal life.* And so forth. In funeral liturgies we ask that the dead may share in the *resurrection of Christ*, that God may *welcome them into his kingdom*, that they may *share his glory, become like God*, and praise him *forever.*

Thus, while the Christian community struggles to make this world a better place, it is at the same time determinedly forward-looking. How could it be otherwise, since the incarnation of the Son of God has interwoven our lives with the eternal? But we will see too that the future is revealed not simply as an object of hope, but to help us shape the present appropriately toward that future. Eschatological belief is to be transformative of our ways of engaging in this world. To know where you are going helps you to decide how to get there.

The Hope You Have in You

As said earlier, Christian assertions about the life to come are based on good evidence but that evidence is obviously not compelling. The reality of the life to come can neither be proved nor disproved. So these pages try to tell the Christian story of the life to come as clearly as possible. Only so, can enquirers choose to believe it. St. Peter urged the first Christians: "Be ready at all times to answer anyone who asks you to explain the hope you have in you, but do it with gentleness and respect" (1 Pt 3:15-16: Good News Version).

I am encouraged by the remark of Balthasar that if the Christian vision in its entirety were presented well, it would have a deeply compelling quality. I hope to offer an integrated alternative to a distorted eschatology which was divorced from other Christian beliefs. To illustrate: the common challenge, "What about hell?" cannot be treated alone. It calls up other questions: "What sort of being is God? What is the nature of divine loving? Who was Jesus? What does salvation mean? Did the resurrection really happen? What about forgiveness? Can the solidarity of humankind and the communion of saints do for sinners what they cannot do for themselves?" Christian belief forms a seamless tapestry, and every truth has a context.

Off Limits?

Biblical revelation offers only broad indicators of what eternal life will be like. But even a small candle lit on a dark night can enable a cautious step in the right direction. At the outset, we must not be reduced to silence by the frequent misinterpretation of the phrase from St. Paul,

"What no eye has seen, nor ear heard, nor the human heart conceived, what God has prepared for those who love him" (1 Cor 2:9).This verse suggests that Paul is saying that speculation on the nature of our future life is "off-limits." But in fact the verse is a quotation from Isaiah (sixth century BC) and hints at the fullness of the Christian revelation which would come later. Paul is saying that this revelation has been made to us just recently through Jesus Christ, and it includes the promise of life after death. It's as if Paul were saying to an interested enquirer,

"You just can't imagine the riches hidden in Christianity; this new faith promises us a new and eternal life! Until Jesus came we knew little about the kindly plans of God for us, but now the mystery of what God is doing for us has been revealed. It is Good News! The life of the world to come is the ultimate fulfillment of this life that we know so well: in it we will meet the author of all love and beauty, where we will be our most lovable selves and see our world in its own radiant glory." It is easy to understand how such preaching created a "buzz" in the early Church, especially among the many poor whose lives were "brutish, short and dull" and, we may add, hopeless.

In these pages we dare to explore together our mysterious future, but not a future totally unknown. Our mentor is God. The revealed future can bring hope and meaning to our lives, enable us to cope better with the challenges we have to face on our journey, and bring new energy to a tired Church.

Your Starting Point

If we were meeting face to face, our discussion would begin where you are at. Starting points differ depending on whether you are a convinced Christian, a Christian agnostic, or an unattached but interested searcher. You may be asking yourself, "Do I believe in God at all?" "Have I any clear ideas on the afterlife?" Perhaps you find that your present position is a mix of confusing beliefs and images. For example, in your view, is God both a loving parent and a stern judge? We live in a world of images, so here and there to lighten the intellectual content I offer hints of an imaginative kind about God and God's dreams for us. As said in the introduction, one of the great characteristics of God is limitless imagination — look at the bio-diversity of nature! A well-educated imagination can help us to touch on the future which God is dreaming of for us.

The Christian Point of Departure

Before we start this mystery voyage into largely uncharted waters, it is good to refresh our understanding of central Christian beliefs. They are both profound and simple:

- God is the being whose name is Love, and who invites us into divine relationship. Our happiness lies in friendship with God.

- Jesus, fully divine and fully human, reveals to us God's loving kindness in concrete human ways and at great personal cost to himself. He shows us that God is totally FOR US.

- The Holy Spirit works in us to make us grow in love with God and one another.

- The Universal Community of Love — divine and human — will be the final achievement of God's labor in human history.

The various chapters of this book will draw out these themes. Our focus throughout will be on God-as-Love and the perpetuation of the relationships in which he has established us through his Son.

A Witness to Hope

Perhaps this humble assertion of hope in eternal life from Karl Rahner, a great theologian of the last century, will resonate with you:

I have this hope of eternal life, even if I cannot actually imagine what it will be like.

I know from Jesus Christ that the absolute, all-embracing, holy, eternally good God has promised himself to me as my future.

Because of that, I have unconditional hope.

This hope is still subject to temptation as long as I am here on earth and I endure negative experiences with life, with society, with people, and so on.

But till death's door I'll hold doggedly to the belief that there is an eternal light and it will illumine me.[12]

Summary

1. Interest in eschatology is weak, due to a legacy of impoverished imagery and explanation.
2. Yet Christian faith is massively future-oriented. Jesus' central promise is "eternal life" and he lived in hope of it himself.
3. Christian eschatology promises the ultimate fulfillment of our freedom.

For Pondering

◊ The title of this book is *Where To From Here?* If you were interviewed today about your hopes for your future, what would you want to say?

---

12. Karl Rahner, *I Remember: An Autobiographical Interview with Meinhold Krauss* (London: SCM, 1985), p. 110.

The Sound of Music

Magic in the Station

An imaginative interlude may help readers who find themselves wary of "heavy theology" to do with the world to come. Recently, a friend directed me to a video clip which moved me deeply and which provides an image of what this book is all about.[13] The location is the concourse of the Central Train Station in Antwerp. Imagine the scene: crowds of people, all going their own way, busy about their affairs, each with their own inner world — the happy, the sad, the serious, the imaginative, the tense, the worried, the practical, the hurried and the relaxed — all are there. Suddenly something totally unexpected breaks in on the occupants of the concourse. First music, then "Do Re Mi" from *The Sound of Music*. Actors in ordinary clothes, both adults and children, begin to dance: more and more join in as the song moves along. Onlookers can't tell actors from spectators, so inhibitions are lowered as people stop what they're busy doing and get in on the act themselves. Children, then adults with the heart of children, join in first. People are drawn out of themselves, some with hands to their mouths in delighted awe. Eventually, the concourse is full of dancers. The core group of actors keeps the rest in synch — well, partly at least, but that doesn't matter. There's space for everyone, whether they're coordinated or not. Nobody's looking critically at how you perform, at your arthritic jig or as you wave your crutch. The outer circle is littered with bags and coats which people have shed in order to dance freely. Maybe the coat and the bag will be stolen, but who cares? On the faces are surprise, disbelief, delight. There are just the odd few with "Silly stuff!" written on their faces, and even they are intrigued. Cell phones and cameras flash so that this ecstatic moment can be recalled and passed on to friends. Laughter and tears of joy mingle with regret that this treasured moment will pass. There is a yearning that it will somehow go on forever.

---

13. *Sound of Music*, Central Station Antwerp Belgium, http://www.youtube.com/watch?v=7EYAUazLI9k , accessed 27 October 2011.

Applause

What has happened? For a few moments, people have been drawn beyond themselves by the beauty of something bigger than they've known before. Hearts have been caught and nourished. The usual boundaries have become porous — people who have never met feel that they're in this together and a common humanity has emerged. Mutual trust has grown as people let themselves go. There is gratitude to the unknown organizers of this moment of joy. Were they to reveal themselves there'd be a crescendo of applause. The crowd would surge forward to shake their hands, to get a photo beside them, to experience their energy and joy. In the excited buzz you hear the questions: do these people find fun in making others happy? Why all this generosity — everyone invited in — not like a theatre where you pay, or like a party for which you need an invitation? What must the orchestrators of this magic be like?

Totally Loved!

Does this passing moment of happiness give a tiny hint of what may await us at the End? Will the human story culminate in a delightful surprise, something which we could never conjure up but which meets the needs of our hungry hearts? Will there be music and dancing then, and will everyone be invited to join in? Will those who know the music and the dance pull in the slow and uncomprehending? Will there be a growing awareness that all material baggage can be let go because it won't be needed anymore? And will inner baggage too be shed — pain, suffering, fear, resentment, jealousy, hatred? Will we leave hold of the primal mistake of thinking that no one really cares about us, and will we find our hearts softened toward others, even enemies? Will we have a sense that it's all right to express our unique selves within the great harmony? Will there be a dawning awareness that we are in an ecstatic moment which will never fade? Might a nagging doubt arise in us: "Am I good enough for all of this?" But we don't have to be "good enough" — it suffices that God is so. You don't get an inheritance because you're good but because the donor is good. Perhaps we will each say: "Oh my God, I'm all right: I'm totally loved!" Will we in all simplicity enjoy ourselves and take joy in others and in God's creation? Will we look back and realize that human life was intended by God as the beginnings of a celebration?

God as Radiant Joy

Suppose now that the authors of this happy surprise appear: they are three, yet one, but somehow this is manageable. They are *themselves* music and dance and joy and harmony and beauty and love. These qualities radiate from them, like sunbeams and warmth from the sun. Their deep attractiveness draws everyone toward them. Somehow they're everywhere, and they meet you and me and all of us just as we are, and we begin to feel totally special. They won't ask to be thanked: their joy is in making everyone else happy. They love without demanding a return, but spontaneously we will burst into shouts of praise and thanks, applause and laughter.

Looking at each other we see recognition, appreciation, acceptance. We become truly at home with everybody else, in the home of the Three who have planned, labored and anguished to fulfill the hope of human history so magnificently. There is no more alienation, no more fear or grief, no wrongdoing, no groups privileged or dominant at the expense of others. We belong equally: there are no outsiders to this joy; everyone is wanted, each makes their unique contribution to the happiness of the others. Even those who used to spoil the happiness of others are mellowed, the best of them will have emerged.

Story Telling

We each tell our story, and all want to hear it: we are amazed how all our stories are intertwined. The most casual happenings, we find, turn out to have had lasting significance — a smile, a kindness, a moment of caring, a suffering patiently endured, a simple prayer. More amazing yet, we discover that even our sin has been woven into something beautiful. Out of the world's seemingly inexhaustible store of evil, overwhelming good has come. As Good Friday is rightly called "good" because the evil of hate was transformed by great love, so every day of human history has become a good day. There is no mastering this mystery, only awed joy in the realization that God has made all things work together for our good. Transformed by all this goodness and love, we become radiant from within and others see and are delighted for us, as we are for them.

All this is hinted at in Scripture, in Christian tradition and the writings of the mystics. We are, after all, loved extravagantly and everlastingly: God's joy will be in us, and "our joy will be complete" (Jn 15:11). So, at the close of history, our surprising destiny will be to share in the glory of the Son who shared our human condition, including death. We will be where he now is (Jn 14: 3). We who weep now are already blessed, for we shall then laugh (Lk 6:21).

Summary

1. We can believe that, at the close of world history, God will intervene in a dramatic and humanly fulfilling way.
2. This divine action will reveal God as pure love, creative, attractive, welcoming to all.
3. We will be drawn beyond ourselves toward God and one another, and our hearts will be filled with happiness and joy that will know no ending.

For Pondering

◊ What images of the world to come do you find satisfying?

Changing Christian Thinking
on the World to Come

Unhelpful Imagery

*H*ow up to date are your images of the world to come? Each Christian generation is faced with the task of forging a deeper understanding of revelation and expressing it in contemporary language. Were Jesus to come on earth today, he would accommodate himself to our mind-set, culture, imagination, vocabulary and technology in presenting his vision of our future. This chapter, then, offers indicators of recent significant shifts within the Christian community in its thinking on eschatology.

Changes

But can there be development in Church teaching? Yes, because our ideas are immersed in history: they are not given to us in their completeness all at once. Vatican II illustrates the progress of faith on many fronts, such as kinder attitudes to those of other denominations and faiths. Over the last two thousand years, Christian understanding about the life of the world to come has changed considerably. Within New Testament times alone, the hope of the imminent return of the risen Jesus yielded to the realization that Christians were instead in for "the long haul." Soon after, the hope of a triumphant *corporate* destiny gave way to concern for individual salvation. Under the influence of St. Augustine, pessimism began to dominate over Christian hope. Fear and terror, born of an exaggerated emphasis on sin and damnation, replaced the confident call with which the New Testament closes: "Come, Lord Jesus!" (Rev 22:20). The sinfulness of humankind eclipsed the greatness and kindness of God.

In the past, Scripture, understandably, was taken literally and its imagery around the end-times gave limitless scope to artists, sculptors, writers, musicians and preachers. A central focus was the Last

Judgment (Mt 25:31-46). The sculptors of the great Irish High Crosses portray the saved heading blissfully to heaven, while demons with tridents prod the damned into hell. The twelfth-century hymn, *Dies Irae*, sung in Masses for the dead until Vatican II, speaks of the return of Christ as "That day of wrath, that dreadful day." Dante's *Divine Comedy*, written about 1300, elaborates in matchless language the details of hell, purgatory and heaven. In 1541, Michelangelo completed his terrifying *Last Judgment* on the wall of the Sistine Chapel. Milton's *Paradise Lost* (1667) made far more impact than his *Paradise Regained* (1671). Later came the classic sermon on hell preached by a Jesuit to the riveted schoolboy James Joyce in *The Portrait of the Artist as a Young Man* (1916). Our solidarity in Christ, giving hope for the salvation of all, was eclipsed by a scramble to save oneself, to "get into heaven" at whatever cost: hence the vast sums donated by the rich for Masses and prayers for "the repose of their souls."

Aggiornamento

Vatican II initiated the task of *aggiornamento,* or updating of Christian thinking. This involved a return to the rich sources of Christian belief. Such research was intended to liberate us from culture-bound images: new thinking and imagery, more faithful to revelation and more satisfying to educated minds, would emerge.[14] This is the program attempted here: to present eschatology afresh, in a way that is faithful to the core of the Christian Scriptures and to the best of Catholic tradition. Vatican I (1869–70), states that we can gain some limited understanding of divine mysteries, and that *this can be most fruitful.* A blind child traces out the physiognomy of his mother's face: it is not the best of knowledge but it is vital. So here too we struggle to make sense of what we do not yet know from experience, in the belief that this can be most fruitful in our search for ultimate meaning in our lives.

No Wild Imagining

The temptation in the past was to let imagination loose on the world to come. As a corrective, consider the following statement from the Vatican:

---

14. See *Lumen gentium,* n. 7.

> When dealing with man's situation after death, one must especially beware of arbitrary imaginative representations: excess of this kind is a major cause of the difficulties that Christian faith often encounters. Respect must however be given to the images employed in the Scriptures. Their profound meaning must be discerned, while avoiding the risk of over-attenuating them, since this often empties of substance the realities designated by the images.[15]

And this reflection from a theologian:

> We are forced to remember that when we have lived out our dark night and passed through the dark exit, we enter into a life that cannot be imagined in any picture, however pretty. Already in this present state our life is one that "is hidden with Christ in God" (Col 3:3), and "what we will be has not yet been revealed" (1 Jn 3:2). The inexplicable silence of those who have gone before us should alert us to the infinite distance that separates our present life from the life to come. As there is no proportion between the nothingness from which we came and the being we enjoy in the present life, so there is no proportion between our natural being and the divine life that is to be ours.[16]

This sober comment from a balanced Catholic scholar advises us to tread cautiously and not to get lost in speculative imagery. Crowe, however, would surely agree with our plan, to explore the resources of Scripture and Christian tradition so that we can present well what God wishes us to know.

Images and Reality

"Granting that the images you use are newer" a friendly critic said to me, "who is to say they're truer? All images become out-dated, so will these newer ones also fade in time?" They may indeed fade. Newman reminds us that the human mind works along with shadows and images until it finally emerges into the full light of truth. "We see now only dimly as in a mirror" (1 Cor 13:12). So let's concede the inadequacy of human thought and language to express the mind of God. Aquinas, who wrote a million words on things divine, said we merely stammer in speaking of God. But at the same time, let's

---

15. Letter on *Certain Questions Concerning Eschatology*, 1979.
16. F. E. Crowe, *Lonergan and the Level of our Time*, ed. Michael Vertin (Toronto: University of Toronto Press, 2010), p. 356.

take heart from Vatican II's image of the pilgrim Church. Pilgrims edge along difficult paths, using all available help to arrive at their destination. At crossroads they discuss the path that seems most promising and they turn back if it fails them. The French theologian, Henri de Lubac, uses the image of swimming: with each stroke you push a volume of water behind you as you move toward your objective, but without that water you would never get there. Think then of these pages, not as presenting "the real thing" but as hinting at it. There is a Zen saying about a farmer pointing to the moon with a carrot. It was the best he could do to get others to see this wondrous reality! As we approach the world of divine mystery, an amber light glows; it does not forbid entry but warns us: "Proceed with caution!"

Recent Thinking on Eschatology

When the medieval map makers had sketched out the limits of the known world, they wrote in the empty spaces beyond: "There be dragons!" The map offered here is small indeed, but in the empty spaces one might write: "There be God!"

1. The Dynamic

New thinking about eschatology sees humankind as in process towards an open goal, rather than working to a blueprint already fixed in the mind of God. With God, we create the temporal and the eschatological future. In the past, the perceived connection between the "Good News" and the "Last Things" was at best ambiguous, but now theologians project from present to future and from future to present.

2. The Relational

Study of the Trinity has blossomed in recent years.[17] Distinct from other religions which understand God as only one Person, Christian belief is that God is Three Persons, who are totally-for-one-another. At the heart of divine reality stand relationships. Further, the Three invite us into their own mode of relating: they are for-us, and we are to be for-one-another and for-them. Christian faith is to

---

17. For an introduction to the work of the Trinity in our lives, see Brian Grogan and Una O'Connor, *Love Beyond All Telling: An Introduction to the Mystery of God* (Dublin: Messenger Publications, 1988).

be understood in terms of divine–human relationships, which are creative, surprising, challenging and ultimately fulfilling. Female theologians such as Catherine M. LaCugna and Elizabeth Johnson, articulate the far-reaching implications of a relational understanding of God.[18] On another level, "Vatican II taught many things, but few more important than the style of relationship that was to prevail in the Church."[19] This relational approach was adopted because it was seen to mirror God's own style of relating with the People of God.

3. The Centrality of Love

> However it happened, the image that was handed down was of a God prying into every nook and cranny of life, and of a Church flushing sin from the coverts of our souls. How did we get from the spring flower of the New Testament to the sick worry of the confessional?[20]

While images of God are always inadequate, some are less distorted than others. The least inadequate image is that "God is Love" (1 Jn 3:8, 16). This revelation is to be our constant reference point. This Being who is simply love always acts out of pure love: so God is always creatively and actively on our side (Rm 8:31).

Thus, we can both assert that God hates sin because it spoils good relationships, and also that God's final action of judgment on the world will match the wonder of all his interventions on our behalf. It will be loving, gracious, creative, redemptive, life-giving, transforming. God's love "does not end" (1 Cor 13:8). All that we value in life and fear to lose will be treasured by God and fulfilled beyond measure.

4. The Pivotal Role of Christ

In the newer thinking about salvation we human beings are no longer the center of anxious attention. What God is doing for us is vastly more important than what we have been up to. Divine grace is

---

18. Catherine M. LaCugna, *God For Us: The Trinity and Christian Life* (San Francisco: Harper, 1973); Elizabeth Johnson, *She Who Is, The Mystery of God in Feminist Theological Discourse* (New York: Crossroad, 1995).

19. John W. O'Malley, *What Happened at Vatican Two* (Cambridge, MA: Harvard University Press, 2008), p. 307.

20. V. McNamara, *The Call to be Human: Making Sense of Morality* (Dublin: Veritas, 2010), p. 90.

emphasized over human waywardness. Christ's centrality is restored through a reclaiming of the notion of solidarity. Just as there is human solidarity in sin, there is divine solidarity in grace. Our corporate triumphal destiny is due to Christ and not to ourselves. We will be saved because God in Christ achieves his kind purposes in us. This emphasis on the glorified Christ in the eschaton in no way diminishes the role of the Father and the Spirit. Each divine Person illuminates a distinct facet of God's engagement with us.

5. Hope for the Salvation of All

As we have noted, literal interpretations of scriptural texts about judgment and punishment infected the Christian imagination and led to fear and uncertainty about the salvation of everyone. A significant change, as we shall see below, is the assertion in the *Catechism of the Catholic Church* (1992) that Jesus' statements about sin and hell are to be understood *not literally,* but as dramatic warnings that we must live relationally rather than as self-centered beings. This approach liberates Christian hope that all may yet be well for us. It is a response to Pope Paul VI's challenge in 1976:

> What has happened to that hidden energy of the Good News? May the world of our time, which is searching, sometimes with anguish, sometimes with hope, be enabled to receive the Good News not from evangelizers who are dejected, discouraged, impatient or anxious, but from ministers of the Gospel who have first received the joy of Christ and who are willing to risk their lives so that the Kingdom be proclaimed.[21]

God intends to bring all to glory: Christian hope, as we shall see, is based on impressive evidence that this extraordinary project will succeed.

6. The Transformation of death

While death retains its fearful dimension, Christ is with us. He does not stand back and leave us to face our darkness unbefriended. Rather his death transforms our dying: "Dying you destroyed our death ..." Our dying can have the dimension of a decision for God, it can be a relational event, an act of communion. Death is a moment

---

21. *Evangelii nuntiandi*, n. 80.

of transition. The meeting with Christ in death is shot through with welcome and love. "We cannot speak any more of 'Last Things,' but only of a face-to-face encounter with the Easter Christ, an encounter that will bring our life to its final consummation."[22]

7. The Limits of Space-Time Categories

The intra-worldly constructs of space and time distort our understanding of the future life and eclipse the centrality of relationships within it. We need to watch out for their intrusion. For example, we don't take a celestial elevator to go *up* to a place called heaven nor *down* to a place called hell; instead, heaven is the ultimate fulfillment of relationships, and hell the failure of relationship with God and others. God is not *in space* but is everywhere, or at the Center if one prefers. To be with God is heaven, to be without God is hell. Nor again are we consigned to purgatory *for a period*, which is why the Church has become cautious in promoting indulgences. Purgatory is heart-time! Nor is eternity simply *an extension of time:* we don't change horses at death and then gallop on forever!

Again Jesus' metaphors — "I am *in* my Father and you *in* me and I *in* you" (Jn 15:20) — and the indwelling of the three Persons are to be understood not spatially but in terms of relationships. The phrase "The Lord is *with* you" is to be taken dynamically: God will support us in what God asks us to do.

Lastly, did humans actually walk with God in the cool of the evening long ago? Is salvation simply a restoration of what we then had? Or can we acknowledge the humble beginnings of the human story some 150,000 years ago and say that the *best is yet to come*? Can we then read the Genesis story as presenting the ideal toward which humankind is still struggling — an open relationship with God, akin to the best of friendship?

8. The Relevance of Future to Present

A Jesuit philosopher once said to me cryptically: "The afterlife? Well, God's got me this far, I guess he'll go the whole way." Many of

---

22. Luis M. Bermejo: *Light Beyond Death: The Risen Christ and the Transfiguration of Man* (Chicago: Loyola Press, 1986), p. 3.

us put the "End Things" on the back burner while we get on with life. To emphasize the point:

> One of the most deplorable expressions ever used in theology... is undoubtedly "The Last Things." Afterlife is not primarily ... an advanced report of things to come... it is rather the future that illuminates the present.[23]

Each eschatological truth relates to daily life. The media tell us *how things are*; the eschaton tells us *how things are meant to be*. The future must challenge and irradiate our present praxis with new meaning and energy. We live like the prisoners in Plato's cave, and we need to be freed in order to live in the light of the real world.[24] While living in this world we are already citizens of the world of the eternal, as St. John reminds us (6:47), so there is continuity between "this life" and the "next." God discloses our future to us so that we may take direction from it *now*. In the eternal dimension everyone is in good relationship, so our present life, in its structures and institutions, should mirror the eternal. The eschaton illuminates all earthly relationships and works to transform them. We pray daily: "Thy will be done *on earth*, as it is in heaven." So this book is a call to present action.

9. Cosmic Relationships

There is a growing sense that "our" world — which is actually God's — has its place in the final scheme of things. For much of Christian history, matter has been suspect, with Platonism stressing the encasement of the immortal soul within the earthbound body. The Hebrew understanding of the unity of the person was eclipsed, and so we were taught that in death the "separated soul" enjoys the beatific vision in heaven, while the resurrected body is added in only at the last day. Now, however, the transformation of matter by the incarnation is emphasized, the unity of the person is acknowledged, and our resurrection is understood as the rising of the total person to life with God. This brings into focus the final transformation of the cosmos. We are "children of this world," in Rahner's term, and God through the incarnation has become forever part of the material

---

23. Luis M. Bermejo, *Light Beyond Death*, p. 1.
24. Plato, *The Republic*, Book Seven.

universe. The cosmos is being transformed through his resurrection, and this invests our ecological concerns with grace and hope.

Summary

1. Christian doctrines are always open to development, because the Holy Spirit leads us into the fullness of truth (Jn 16:13).
2. Outworn ideas and images must be replaced by those which less inadequately reflect what God reveals to us.
3. The concept of relationship is key to the nature of God as Trinity, and is central to all Christian living, now and hereafter.
4. Eschatology is relevant to every dimension of life in the here and now.

For Pondering

◊ Which outworn images of the world to come do you need to let go? What new ones do you want to invest in?

- PART TWO -

The Divine Project

Graced Relationships

What are Relationships?

Relationships, we have said, are key to understanding the eschaton: what God intends is the emergence and free flow of graced relationships in this world, which will be perfected in the next. But what are relationships?

Although they cannot be subjected to scientific analysis, relationships are impressively real. We can think of them in terms of "presence." Evolutionary development can be characterized as an ever-increasing complexity of modes of presence. Thus, stones in a heap have a spatial presence to one another but no more, whereas stones in a wall have a basic level of interdependence. Sheep have a humble mode of presence to one another, while dogs are actively present to their owners. We humans have highly developed modes of mutual presence: physical, social, affective, emotional, intellectual, volitional, spiritual. We can love, form friendships, create lasting family life, undertake great projects together, sacrifice ourselves for others. We use the internet, cell phones and email to keep in touch, we lament the absence of those we love. When two good people love each other deeply, we speak of their presence to each other in terms of a union of heart and soul. We are, in short, made for relationships.

Koinonia

When we bring God into the equation, relationship and mutual presence are raised to a new level. We are present to God by being created and sustained by him. The Hebrews became aware that Yahweh was inviting them into a relationship which would secure their well-being in this world. God had set his heart on them out of pure love: they were asked to respond in loving gratitude.

The "Good News" that Jesus brings is that God has gone yet further in the depth of presence that he opens up for us. We find that the Author of our world is characterized in terms of relationships:

God is revealed not as a unitary being but as three-Personed. We are Trinitarians! This of itself would not bring us closer to God, but the astonished joy of the early Christians was to realize that they were themselves invited into the interpersonal relationships revealed in God. So we find ourselves already within the community of divine Persons. Being human is not a barrier to this: we are "adopted" into the divine family. This new set of relationships is called the *koinonia*, a Greek word which means "fellowship" or "fellowship by intimate communication" (Latin: *communio*). "We declare to you what we have seen and heard so that you also may have *fellowship* with us; and truly our *fellowship* is with the Father and with his Son Jesus Christ" (1 Jn 3:2). *Koinonia* will be an important word throughout these pages: it underpins the reality of terms such as People of God, Church, Body of Christ, Christian Community, Communion of Saints, and Community of Love.[1] "Fellowship" connotes respect, equality and bondedness. Fellowship with the Trinity in no way inhibits or frustrates our desire for the fullness of life; rather the divine Persons complete that desire beyond our wildest imaginings.

The importance of the *koinonia* for today is illustrated in a simple way by a study of the decline of socializing in the US. Robert D. Putnam's *Bowling Alone* shows that Americans are becoming more and more isolated from one another, and hence less happy, healthy and safe.[2] But this extensively researched book ends with threadbare solutions to the decline of the community, such as educational programs and work-based social initiatives. The *koinonia* is the divine solution, already operative, to the endemic mutual hostility that leads to the fragmentation of societies.

The *koinonia* grows through a mutual commitment which embraces the human and the divine. In the days of the death squads, the Christians of El Salvador and Argentina developed in their liturgy a dramatic way to celebrate their faith, hope and resistance. When the community had assembled, the list of the disappeared would be read out, and, one by one, someone would stand and say for the person

---

1. For a rich development of the term "Community of Love," see Joseph Papin, ed., *The Eschaton: A Community of Love* (Villanova: Villanova University Press, 1971).

2. Robert D. Putnam, *Bowling Alone* (New York: Simon & Schuster, 2001).

named: *"Presente!"* The "disappeared" indeed were present: each had a unique name and dignity, and had a voice still, through the mouths of their caring sisters and brothers. The congregation drew strength and courage from the three divine Persons to continue to build the *koinonia* in their troubled country despite the risk of brutal death.

The Network of Grace

If relationships can be understood in terms of "presence," what about Grace? Grace is an umbrella term or a code word used by the early Church to cover all that is involved in God's loving action on our behalf through Jesus Christ. Grace points to the transcendent and dynamic relationships which engage our human reality to its fullest, including our bodies and the material world.

All Christian "truths" are to be understood in terms of grace, that is, in terms of our relationship with God and others. So in the life of the *koinonia*, that divine–human community which God is establishing, the symbols and rituals which we call sacraments are not "things" but aspects of our relationship with God and one another. For example, we say that in the Eucharist the bread and wine become "the Body and Blood" of Christ, but that conveys only inadequately the fact that through them we meet the living Christ in person.

Likewise for all the sacraments: they are essentially interpersonal encounters. God in Christ comes through them to meet us, and we are enabled to inch forward towards what we are intended to be. Our continuing focus in dealing with each eschatological reality will be on *the relationships involved*. Thus, for example:

- Dying is to be understood not simply as a terminal reality that we share with animals, but rather as our meeting with a loving and caring God.

- Purgatory is not a place of punishment, but a redeeming engagement with Jesus, who heals the waywardness of our divine and human relationships.

- Sin is not just disobeying a rule but the wounding of the delicate fabric of human and divine relationships. In sinning I hurt myself, others and God. I distort reality as it is meant to be.

- Forgiveness of sin means the restoration of relationships rather than an act of personal hygiene.

- Hell is not a place of eternal torture devised by a vengeful deity, but would be the consequence of a chosen definitive rupture in relationships between an individual and all other persons, human and divine.

- Heaven is not a place somewhat better than earth, but the lasting and dynamic fulfillment of the relationships of love for which we are destined.

- Salvation is not a private accomplishment, but, we may hope, a divine achievement embracing everyone.

- Final human fulfillment is a cosmic celebration of relationships, born of ecstatic joy in God, oneself and in all others.

Since this book is written from a Christian perspective, we will be unfolding the implications of the graced relationships revealed in the New Testament.

The Dynamics of Grace

Grace is the project of a loving God in Christ, active within the network of human relationships. Thus, it is not a purely "spiritual" event but concretely located within our world. An image of it is the United Nations Assembly, with its visionary goal of universal justice and concord. Grace is active within all systems that work for the good of humankind, since its concern is to promote an all-embracing network of healthy and loving relationships. Its ultimate goal is the reconciliation of all humankind.

Grace is intended as a collaborative venture between God and ourselves. Concerned for the good of everyone, it works without arsenal, army or budget. Its only weapon is love. The peace it intends is one which everyone can enjoy because each is included and respected. Grace knows nothing of domination or self-interest or exclusion. Its care extends to all material creation as a precious gift to be protected. Its origins are divine, not human: this is why we rightly hope and pray that it will ultimately succeed in its purpose. It is not a spectator event: each of us has a unique role to play in forwarding it.

A Family Celebration

A simple image can illustrate the dynamics of grace. Imagine a very good couple: they take great delight in one another and never get bored when together. They do their very best for each other. In time they become the happy parents of a wonderful son. He is their delight: they're head over heels about him. They lavish love on him and he responds: he is happy in pleasing them. This nuclear family has wonderful years together. Blessed with enough of the world's goods and by the quality of their relationships, they have all they need to be happy.

But they have been taking notice of the lives of people around them, who all seem to be missing something that would make them truly happy. So they decide to open up their home and to share their happy family life with outsiders. Their son readily agrees to invite people into a celebration. But the poorer people around find it hard to understand their invitation. They feel inadequate, and afraid that they'd be made to feel even smaller than they already are. Self-made folk judge that they might lose something: "No such thing as a free lunch," they say. Life is a matter of deals, and there's a hidden risk here somewhere. So they decline. In the long run the son wins the friendship of only a few — quite a mixed bag — and brings them home. When these people ask him if they will have to be on their best behavior, he laughs and says, "You only have to be yourselves, and try to be easy with whoever else is there." He adds, "There's a good atmosphere in our home. You'll like it, it's simple. Everyone is *for* everyone else, and that's about it!"

Of those who take up the invitation, some become totally at home and enjoy themselves and everyone else's company. Others drift off after a while because they find it too demanding to be "for" the others. They're centered on themselves, and being "for" others is beyond them. Yet it bothers them that the others there are so happy. Those who like to dominate find they just don't belong. But those who had lived oppressed lives find that now they're free just to be themselves. They blossom and develop and their best qualities emerge. Their only worry is that the celebration will soon end. But when they check this out with the son, he says it's an open-ended event: there's no need to go away, and there are rooms for everyone.

The news spreads and crowds come along and join in. Soon the dominating types in the area find that their power base is evaporating. They try to negotiate with the son, then find fault with what he's doing — all this stuff about being for others won't work, they say. Fearing a social revolution which will leave them adrift, they judge it best — for the common good, of course — to maintain order by killing the son. They trump up false charges against him and then kill him brutally, as a warning to his adherents. His parents are horrified, but their response amazes everyone: they keep their home open, even to their son's enemies. They do this because they are committed to their son's message about *being for others* — he, after all, had learned it from them.

Next, mysterious rumors began to spread that the son was alive again! "How could that be?" people wondered. They worked it out that it was because he had died willingly for everyone, good and bad. That kind of love, it seemed, is so pure that it conquers death. Then people began to find that the good spirit of the family was affecting them and indeed overtaking them, in a gentle and profound way. They began to live as the son had done, and became witnesses to him. They sometimes suffered in spreading what they called "the Good News" because their hearers just couldn't handle it, but their joy was infectious. The buzz grew and grew. "Life as we knew it has been turned upside down," people said. "Now we have hope: in fact life is a celebration." Then they said, "Those folk are just so good. This whole thing from beginning to end is pure gift!" And so they adopted the term "grace" to describe it.

"But is it True?"

Our little fable is drawn from the pages of the New Testament:

1. The three divine Persons are in perfect relationships with one another. They share an infinite happiness together; they have no need of anything to complete it (Jn 5:20; Mk 1:11; Jn 16:14; Jn 8:29 etc.). They are totally for-one-another, as three great friends, or a happy nuclear family.

2. The three divine Persons are so happy that they decide to create humankind and to draw them into their own happiness. We

see this process in the fisherman Peter when Jesus steps into his world. Jesus, the son in our story, is a man like Peter, except that he carries a secret. He knows that he himself is totally loved by God, and he wants to share this happiness with Peter.

Soon Peter is aware that there is something very special and different about this man who invites him into friendship. He senses that a new kind of love breaks in on him: it is limitless and unconditioned. Now friends share with one another what they have and are. So Peter shares his boat with Jesus, while Jesus makes promises to Peter, especially that Peter will become a member of the divine family (Jn 10:10).

By becoming Jesus' friend, Peter is introduced into the world of the divine. Peter grows in love with Jesus' best friends. Since Father, Son and Spirit are now totally *for* Peter, he is invited to be totally *for* them.

3. Now notice how *you too* are the focus of the same intense divine love as Peter experienced. You too are limitlessly loved, brought into divine friendship. A whole new set of relationships embrace you. This should make you happy, which is what the Trinity intends! (Jn 16:27; Jn 15:9; Jn 15:13; 1 Jn 3:1; Rm 5:5; Rm 8:16; Rm 8:26).

Note that this love through which the Trinity commit themselves to you is costly for them. The Father sends his Son on a mission which will mean his death. The Son gladly endures his passion for you (Gal 2:20), and the Father suffers in the Son's passion. The Son also suffers when we suffer, because we are his body. And when we do not respond to the call to love, we can "quench" and "grieve" the Spirit (Eph 4:30; 1 Th 5:19). When we wonder whether God suffers, the answer lies here.

Peter and you are invited to respond to the love of the Three for you. This is a work in process! We are asked to love God totally (Mt 23:37; Jn 21:15-17).

4. Loving a good God may not seem too difficult. But the five-fold set of relationships is not yet complete! The guests in our story were told that only one request would be made of them — to accept whoever else showed up at the celebration!

The divine Persons love everyone else as they love me. Now I have to love my neighbor with the same non-calculating love. "Love one another as I have loved you" (Jn 15:12), and "He laid down his life for us — and we ought to lay down our lives for one another" (1 Jn 3:16). The love they give me is indeed mine, and will not be taken away from me. Yet it is for sharing. It is not just for myself but is a reservoir in my heart, waiting to be poured out on others. I must not block the flow of divine love in a needy world, lest the hearts of others wither for lack of it. I am to be an escort of grace to my needy neighbor. Jesus does not define who my neighbor is: instead he turns the issue around and commands that I be a neighbor! He tells the story of a Samaritan who acts as a neighbor by helping an enemy — a Jew — in his need. Then he says to me: "Go and do likewise!" (Lk 10: 37).

I can't wait for my neighbor to love me! If I do, the space between us may never be bridged. Mine must be a creative and often costly love, as is God's love of me. Parents and friends have been loving me with the love given them by God, long before I began to love them. They were my escorts of grace, and I am grateful to them. But there are others who don't love me at all, nor do I love them! And yet my love, like a small rope, must be cast out to them: I must wish them well, and not demand a responding rope from their side of the divide. People are fragile and have perhaps a tangled history which makes loving very difficult for them.

The social boundaries I so carefully nurture must melt, and so too must all forms of domination and control of others. What we call "heaven" will be the fulfillment of all relationships, the final community of love. There, God accepts everyone, and so shall I.

Enemies Too?

We must add that our love is to extend even to our enemy. This is a radical shift from Old Testament thinking in which enemies were to be eliminated. Love of enemies is specific to Christianity (Mt 5:43-48; 18:21-35). It is a shocking demand, but it is dramatically revealed in the passion and resurrection of Jesus (Lk 23:34; Rm 12:20). He witnesses in his dying to the fact that this dimension of love is intrinsic to divine loving. For us, then, it cannot be seen as impossible or an optional extra!

Summary

1. The simple word "for" signifies what grace is all about. We are all to be *for* one another, as God is *for* us. Enemies are specially included.
2. *Koinonia* is the five-fold fellowship which potentially embraces me and all others. It is the new world order established by Jesus. The *koinonia* is in embryo the Final Community of Love and is the bridge between this world and the world to come.
3. The kingdom of heaven is already in process and is visible in Jesus. We help it to advance by loving one another.

For Pondering

◊ Survey the network of relationships in which you find your-self. Then ask yourself: how many people think of you as someone who is *for* them?

Love of Another Kind

*F*ollowing from the previous chapter, we can ask what the specific quality of this love is that enfolds us in graced relationships? The love that is at the heart of the Good News is a special kind of love, not to be confused with what often passes for love. This "love of another kind" is what carries the project of God toward completion through all the ups and downs of human history. The TV news carries its share of bad news as well as covering issues which seem remote from us. But God is active in all of this, and it can help to ask: "Can I see any signs of divine love at work deep down here?"

The Greeks had distinct words for differing kinds of love:

eros: *Eros* denotes romantic, emotional and sexual love. This love depends on the goodness of the person loved: it is exhilarating – the lover gets a lot from it. But it depends on things going well – if the beloved does not meet my expectations it may disappear. So people fall in love and then break up. A lasting relationship cannot depend on this kind of love, though a deeper love may well include the best of erotic love.

philia: *Philia* denotes the love that characterizes friendship or good fellowship. People experience it when they enjoy one another's company. It is based on mutuality and it bonds groups and communities. So someone says, "I like these people, they respect me and we get along well. Look at all we have achieved together!" But again, *philia* is vulnerable to changing situations and moods. "I'll never go to my bridge club again after what he said last night!" "We were the best of neighbors but now I can't stand her!" *Philia* is vital to human society: *phil*anthropy means love/goodwill toward people; Philadelphia means love of brothers! But again, something deeper is needed to sustain *philia* when the going gets tough.

agape (pronounced *agapay*): When the New Testament speaks of God's love for us, and the love we are meant to have for

one another, it does not use *eros* or *philia* but *agape*. There is
a quantum leap in moving from *eros* and *philia* to *agape* love.
Prior to New Testament times, *agape* love denoted the love
that underpins good family life. Good parents simply love one
another and their child, through good and ill. Unlike *eros* and
philia, *agape* love is not dependent on changes in the beloved. It
is unconditional. So in marriage, couples promise to love one
another for richer, for poorer, for better, for worse — a huge
promise which can only be sustained by a deep, unchanging
and committed love. This love mirrors the faithful love of
God (Hebrew: *hesed*) for wayward Israel.

Unconditional Love

Agape love is the term adopted by the first Christians to best denote
the sort of love God has for us. *Agape* love over-arches but includes
eros and *philia*, because it is based, not on the perceived goodness of
the other, but on a commitment to love the other, no matter what.
Indeed, the worse the situation of the beloved, the more *agape* love
will come into play. In essence it is inexhaustible; in God it is truly
so. Since *agape* love is not a reaction to the goodness of the other, it
survives even in a hostile environment of aggression, malice, hurt-
ful action or alienation. Other levels of love are tinged with anxiety
because they are not fully in our control, but *agape* love is free of
anxiety: it is the fruit of a free decision, so it can survive anything.
Just as God's love for us is independent of hostility and sinning, so
our love is to become independent of the merits of the other. This
insight brings liberation and a level of calm, especially in fraught
situations where otherwise all seems lost. One-sided loving is tough
but blessed. It has a divine quality!

Thus, *agape* love expresses the quality of the Father's love when he
sent his Son into our world, despite knowing that he would be rejected
and killed. Jesus' willingness to die for us is also best expressed by
agape love. The Spirit shows the same quality of love by residing
permanently in our hearts. Trinitarian love is *agape* love, and when
St. John says that God is love, he means, not some vague goodwill
extrapolated from human ways of loving, but *agape* love. This love

bursts in on an unsuspecting world, as the divine remedy for the human predicament. Left to ourselves, we cannot love as we ought, but when we are given *agape* love, which is the virtue of charity, we can live rightly even in a diseased world.

Each of us without exception is loved intensely with *agape* love, and always will be. God gives us this love directly and through others. Where the intended escort of God's *agape* love fails in their task to someone, God works to send others, so that all of us may be sustained by this love. We may never know who some of the escorts are, but the reality of the *koinonia* assures us that we are supported by the free love of countless others, whether they are living in this world or the next.

This love transcends death. "Love is stronger than death" (Songs 8:6-8). *Agape* love does not come to an end (cf. 1 Cor 13:8 — the whole chapter is a hymn to *agape* love). It is this love which gives us sure and certain hope of eternal life with God. God does not stop loving us at death. Awareness that we are loved with *agape* love is transforming, because true love changes people, and *agape* love changes us very deeply. Our secret mantra might be: "I'm loved with *agape* love!" This would cut our psychotherapy bills! When we believe it, we become easier about ourselves: I don't have to be perfect to be loved. This in turn leads to deep gratitude to the One who loves us so.

A Love for Sharing

To be Christian means to be free from basic anxiety about ourselves and our acceptability to God. No longer need we irritate God by moaning "No one loves me!" Aware that we are loved limitlessly, we are now to love others in the same way. Therefore:

- We are to be radiant centers of a love which is without limits, non-discriminating, non-partisan, vulnerable, costly. *Agape* love goes further than is reasonable: it is a costly decision to live out of such love, because its demands are unpredictable.

- Our love is not to be measured by the limited goodness or the reaction of the other. It is generous, not restricted to "deserving cases." Mother Teresa used tell how money came flooding into her from every part of the world. "If I were to hoard it" she would say "it would grow stale in me. Of all that is given to me, all is to be given away." Such generosity is a sign that *agape* love is at home.

• Our love is to be measured by the quality of divine loving. "Just as I have *agape* love for you, you also should *agape* love one another" (cf. Jn 13:34)

• When we act out of *agape* love we create the right environment for *eros* love and *philia* love as described above.

• We have spoken of love of enemies: this is central to Christianity because Christianity is founded in *agape* love. That is why Jesus could tell us to *agape* love our enemies (Mt 5:42). Other than in this context, the term "enemy" should have no place in the Christian vocabulary. Such forgiving love is impossible for the human heart left to itself. It has become possible in our world only because it is poured into our hearts from its divine source. It became incarnate at a certain point in history, in the life, passion, death and resurrection of Jesus. Only then could we fully see just what it involves. But it is for sharing: loved and forgiven ourselves, we are in turn to act toward others with the same love.

• If *agape* love seems in short supply in the world, don't blame God! But in fact it is there, and it flourishes hiddenly, even among those who never hear the term. It is like the Kingdom of God, which according to Jesus, "grows we know not how." As we have seen, the term was first applied to the love that characterizes family life at its best. But everyone knows of good families, whether their own or those of others. There are perhaps one billion families across the world today: many of them carry the flame of *agape* love in a remarkable way. Think also of medical personnel, carers, people who serve others well, voluntary workers, those who struggle for justice, those who pray for the world, and you see that this *agape* love is part and parcel of human living, and holds it together. *Agape* love is not beyond our reach! Nature hints at this love, as when animals sacrifice themselves to save their young, and more universally in the giving and receiving which is the rhythm of the universe.

- *Agape* love and our resurrection from death go together. "We have passed from death to life, because we *agape* love one another" (1 Jn 3:14). We die interiorly or slip towards nothingness when we turn away from God who is Life. Lack of love is the root of sin and its consequence, death. *Agape* love is the antidote to death. Look into your own heart and acknowledge that at least sometimes you act out of a love that is disinterested, pure, steady. Notice the joy it brings. In those moments you are not self-concerned or perturbed about a possibly poor response from the other person. So far as this kind of loving goes on in you, you are becoming like God, you are a carrier of divine love, breathing the air of eternal life.

- When friendship is at its best, it becomes *agape* love. Again, we all experience friendship, see it around us, and cherish it when it emerges in our lives. It is a vital human reality. St. Thomas Aquinas held that true Christian relationships are in fact manifestations of friendship. True friends love one another, no matter what. Mutual appreciation constantly grows; forgiveness is generously given. As far as possible, all life is shared — values, interests, other friends, time, goods, joys and sorrows. Equality prevails; there is no domination. Aristotle could not acknowledge the possibility of friendship between God and humans because of their disparity, but Aquinas' response was that God raises us up to equality with Godself, and so friendship can flourish between us. Jesus says: "I have called you *friends*" (Jn 15:15). Jesus loves me with *agape* love: I can love him in the same way.

All of the above makes it clear that the divinely intended future of humankind is already operating in our world. What will be heard as a crescendo at the End can already be heard now, if we have ears to hear.

Thinking of how the Church can understand itself relationally, Steve Summers writes:

> Those whom one sits next to at the table, or kneels beside at the altar-rail in the Eucharist, are not friends in a notional sense but in a real sense — they are fellow instantiators of *koinonia*, sharing in the gift of God's Spirit. Those who are not yet friends, but may

become so, await a hospitable welcome in the community that is both now and not yet.[3]

We will continue this theme further below, but first we must study the evidence for the resurrection of Jesus, without which the panorama we have been unfolding fades away to nothingness.

Summary

1. God's love involves a commitment to the well-being of humankind which is unaffected by human malice or hostility.
2. Such love is called *agape* love. It is selfless and unconditioned.
3. Our growth in love is to be measured against *agape* love, of which Jesus is the human exemplar.

For Pondering

◊ Recall some persons who have shown you this "love of another kind." Is your own heart expanding in this direction?

---

3. Steve Summers, *Friendship: Exploring its Implications for the Church in Postmodernity* (London: T&T Clark, 2009), p. 194.

"He is Risen!"

Divine Initiative

*T*he case for believing in the life of the world to come stands or falls on the reality of Jesus' resurrection. St. Paul admitted this long ago: "If Christ has not been raised, then our proclamation has been in vain, and your faith has been in vain ... If for this life only we have hoped in Christ, we are of all people most to be pitied" (1 Cor 15:12-19).

"On the third day he rose again." Such is the bald statement in the Creeds. But is it true? How did belief in Jesus' resurrection originate? And even if Jesus rose, how can that give hope that out of the disasters and shame of history, humankind too will be freed from death? Since this book already sketches out a vast terrain, we will not attempt here to pick our way through the academic debate over the resurrection of Jesus. That work fills libraries and scholarly journals. In outlining our case for Jesus' resurrection, let us acknowledge that we humans are totally out of our depth in talking about it, because it is a divine initiative. The best place to start, therefore, is from God's viewpoint rather than our own.

A Bolt from Heaven

The resurrection is the following through of God's decision to love the world with *agape* love (cf. Jn 3:16). God's consequent action is not to be seen as a jarring and undesired intervention in our closed human world. The resurrection instead is a decisive step forward in history, the divine solution to the human inability to achieve sustained progress toward the good. The resurrection and the Gospel miracles are anticipations and hints of the final ordering of things. The curtain is drawn back, and through these windows we can glimpse our intended future.

The challenge God faced after the passion of Jesus was how to convince the world that divine love is eternal and conquers even death, and that, against all reason, the torture and murder of the Son gives us entry into eternal life and joy. God knew that the disciples alone would be hard to convince, not to speak of those outside the Jesus circle. These disciples had indeed seen that Jesus had a certain mastery over death: the widow's son, Jairus' daughter and Lazarus were restored to life. But they were shattered by the fact that Jesus himself had been overcome by the power of death. The all-too-human hopes they had centered on him were in ruins, as they admit on the Emmaus road (Lk 24:21). If they were to come to believe that in *dying lovingly* he had overcome death and was still with them, they would need overwhelming evidence.

So the divine decision was that Jesus — the same, yet different — would encounter the disciples in their ordinary lives and gently draw the veil so that gradually they would recognize him and take on board the tremendous implications of his resurrection.

The resurrection of Jesus was planned by God, not by disciples trying to retain their credibility after their master had been done away with. For them the event was totally unexpected, a bolt from the blue: it took them a long time to accept that their leader had somehow broken through death and was still with them. Caught totally off guard, the disciples only slowly became convinced that something dramatic had occurred which would blow apart their notions of what human life was truly about. "Something has happened" they came to say "which is not myth, not human conspiracy nor poetic imagining!" (cf. 2 Pt 1:16). Excited as never before, they formed a community held together by the fact that they had all been bowled over by the same event.

The Gospel Confusion

The disciples tried to articulate what they had come to believe, and so the Gospels began to form. But as a unique divine event with no parallels, the resurrection is strictly inexpressible: human language is not up to the task. Scholars have dissected the evidence endlessly, and will continue to do so. Critics argue that the discrepancies in the various accounts indicate that the event is a fabrication. But the contradictions only emphasize that this was not a well-thought-out deception. Instead, the disciples were bewildered at what had taken place, and it is no wonder their accounts are garbled. We must not look for too much harmony in the texts, because the harmony is on a higher level — the level of the divine as it breaks in on the human. All the stories are like musical variations on a single theme: "He is risen!" The articulations of this event — which is set on the uttermost borders of human history — fall short of what the searching mind would like, but enough is given to ground the faith of those who choose to believe.

The Empty Tomb

Resurrection at all was a highly debated issue for the scholars of Jesus' day. Jewish martyrs had stated their belief in a resurrection at the close of history (cf. 2 Macc 7) but resurrection in the *middle* of history was unthought of. The disciples, already disoriented by the death of their trusted leader, were now asked to cope with an even more disorienting reality — that he had been raised from the dead! How were they brought to believe this?

The empty tomb was a start, but an empty tomb does not prove that the corpse once placed in it is alive again, and more importantly, it gives no grounds for believing that the once-dead person is still connected with those he loved in life and that he intends to bring them to where he is (see Jn 14:3). The empty tomb and the missing body were divine hints that something dramatic was afoot, but were not enough to convince the disciples of the Grand Plan of the world's redemption.

We Met Him!

Instead, the disciples' faith in the resurrection of Jesus was based on the encounters they had with him. They say they met him, not once but over and over — in the Garden, in the Supper Room, at the Lakeside, in an Emmaus inn. The Gospels grew — backwards as it were — from these stories. As for the nature of these encounters between the risen Lord and the disciples, they are outside our experience. But as Balthasar says, we must not spiritualize their massive realism. While we do not know exactly how Jesus communicated himself, we know that the disciples were transformed in body, mind, heart, soul and spirit. They became focused and galvanized around their Lord even more than they had been when he was on this side of the grave. The encounters impacted on them in a way that they found utterly convincing. What was beyond time and space had invaded their time and space. It is not for us to set norms for how this unique encounter of the divine with the human, the eternal with the temporal, should take place. The tensions in the Scripture texts are deliberate:

- It is dark yet the sun has risen
- The risen Lord is not to be touched, yet they are to feel his wounds
- They do not recognize him, then again they do
- He is both the same and different
- He no longer has a body limited like theirs, yet he takes their food
- He drops in on them and yet disappears as suddenly
- He moves freely from his world into theirs
- Always he chooses the time and place
- They are in despair, yet their hearts begin to burn
- They are told not to seek the Living One among the dead
- They believe, yet they are upbraided for their slowness of heart
- Frightened, confused and uncertain though they are, he commissions them to spread his Good News to all humankind.

These tensions help to situate the encounters on the border between God's world and the world we innocently think of as "ours," but is of course primarily God's. Jesus is shown as totally free in himself, and he respects the freedom of the disciples. He does not overload them with evidence. He could have performed some earth-shattering feat or dramatically vindicated himself before his enemies. But instead he thinks out human ways to enable the truth of his resurrection to dawn upon them. Slowly their lives will be changed, but forever. He holds faith with his beloved disciples and invites them in turn to have faith in him. And so the disciples are gradually convinced by a blend of outer and inner evidence. His message is of peace, he brings consolation and he sends them out as he had done before, but now clothed with new power. They are now within the *koinonia* or five-fold set of relationships comprising Father, Son, Spirit, themselves and those to whom they are sent.

Peter

Let's try to get into the mind of Peter, the leader of the little band of disciples. Before he bumped into Jesus, Peter, a married and not overly-successful fisherman, may have had vague hope of something beyond death, but he had no convincing argument to ground his speculation, even if he sided with the Pharisees against the Sadducees on the point. A few short years later, however, this same man is totally convinced that Jesus has not only risen from the dead, but has opened up the world of God to us and invited us to join him there. What won him over was meeting Jesus in risen form. Peter would have gone back over Jesus' predictions of his violent death but also of his rising "on the third day" (Mt 20:18-19 etc.). He would also have recalled Jesus' promises of "eternal life" to his followers. Now, he saw, these puzzling memories had come to dramatic fulfillment. For him the resurrection of Jesus and all it connotes emerged as a divine action which breaks open the human story and gives hope that we are indeed destined, not for extinction, but for eternal life with God. He and his tiny group did not concoct this: instead they sensed that the divine had irrupted into their dim minds and wavering hearts and mercifully blown to pieces the dull predictability of life. This, for Peter, is overwhelmingly "Good News" which changes everything. Peter emerges drained from the passion, but is now so convinced about Jesus' resurrection that he will take on the world and even die for him.

The Book of Evidence

The evidence for Jesus' resurrection is persuasive but not overwhelming: it can neither be proved nor disproved scientifically. The disciples had a personal decision to make, like jurors faced with a limited amount of evidence in a trial. They were able to give solid arguments for their belief, but it was not a solely intellectual conviction: they were so totally transformed that they gave their lives to share the Good News with an incredulous world. The change in the disciples from cowardice to commitment is impossible to discredit from a historical standpoint. While they did not fully understand their own message — it was too profound for them — they believed, because they had met him, that their master was indeed risen. Their reasons for this belief were, at least to themselves, compelling, and were vindicated over and over by what happened when they lived out their belief. Conviction grew with success, as is the human way. Read the Acts of the Apostles from this point of view. Amazing things happened. People listened and were converted; true community got under way; the sick were healed; prison doors opened; their worst enemy, Saul, was won over; joy, hope and energy flowed as more and more people believed the Message.

The graced side of the history of Christianity shows that for those who truly accept that Jesus is risen, everything is changed and made new. Hope replaces cynicism and despair: the sadness of existence begins to throb with divine mystery; *agape* love displaces hate and violence, authentic relationships bind our fractured world together: meaning displaces futility, and weak persons accomplish what seems humanly impossible. The following chapter elaborates on *our own experience* of the resurrection.

Summary

1. The resurrection of Jesus is a divine initiative, bewildering to the disciples. They are "slow to believe" (Lk 24:25).
2. Jesus' personal encounters with the disciples convinces them that he is indeed risen.
3. Reasonable Christian belief in the world to come depends on the truth of the resurrection.

For Pondering

◊ Do you think that life takes on a new quality when/if one believes in the resurrection?

We Too Can Arise!

All About Us!

There is a Cartier advertisement for a beautiful and expensive ring: the caption is, "All about you, forever." Jesus' resurrection was not understood by the first Christians solely as a vindication or triumph for Jesus who had performed his task so faithfully. Instead, they saw it also as being God's greatest and kindest gift *for us*. They said: "The life, death and resurrection of Jesus is all about us, forever!" The Father might well have raised Jesus from the dead, taken him back to himself and wreaked vengeance on those who had killed him. But Jesus' resurrection is not a dramatic display of divine power, nor an act of vengeance. Instead, its message is pure graciousness on God's part: we too will rise with Jesus!

If you accept the resurrection, everything in life is reframed. To the outside eye things seem to go on as before, but in fact they now lie within a different dimension: human horizons are transposed into the divine one. The resurrection demands that we "think outside the box" about everything, just as God does. Injustice, cruelty, suffering and death continue to wreak havoc, yet because of the resurrection, to adapt Yeats's phrase, "all's changed, changed utterly; a glorious beauty is born." The Latin poets of Jesus' time viewed dying as being plunged into dark and perpetual night. But because of the Jesus event, mortal darkness yields to the delicate life-giving light of early dawn, the inauguration of a new age. This new age is the final or eschatological era in which the caring plans of God for humankind move to climactic completion. We have noted in the resurrection narratives the contrasts of dark and light, of sadness and joy — hints that the old is bathed in the new, the human in the divine.

For the first disciples, the reinterpretation of life's meaning was achieved only with great labor; it was always a business of "catching up" because the event was too big to be controlled. We too are invited to recast, with similar labor, our hopes and our ways of seeing and acting. Like a lighthouse, the resurrection illuminates the past, present and future dimensions of human history. We summarize here some of these aspects: they are elaborated elsewhere throughout these pages.

New Love

The quality and breadth of divine love is made known to us through the paschal mystery, the great deed of God in Christ. We now know that God is *agape* love, that God has no enemies. We can now believe that truly God's love is a forgiving love, and that sin is not an ultimate barrier to relationship with God.

We are to measure up to this New Love. Since God's love is creative and forgiving, we in turn must love and forgive all others, with no exclusions. Hence the term "a new creation," used by Paul to describe the change in those who accept and live out the resurrection (cf. 2 Cor 5:17; Gal 6:15). All relationships are reframed in the *koinonia*: we are all now daughters and sons of God, members of the primordial community of Father, Son and Spirit.

Eternal Life Opens Up

Human life is shown to have ultimate value. Death remains, but becomes a moment of passage into eternal life. We live in a provisional world undergoing the birth-pangs of the resurrection. Continuing personal identity is promised us by the nature of Jesus' resurrection: he is indeed transformed, yet he is the same, and so too will we be. As C. S. Lewis says, in the end our friends will gaze on us with amazed recognition. We will be our full selves, and at our best, forever.

Suffering Has New Meaning

The suffering which disfigures our world seems futile and negative, but is now woven by God into the eternal scheme of things. "Was it not right that the Christ should suffer and so enter his glory?" (Lk 24:26). The "Dynamic of the Cross" (*Lex crucis*) becomes a shorthand for saying that unavoidable suffering, patiently endured, is not wasted but transformed: now it is redemptive and rich with eternal meaning. How do we know this? Because God is shown through the passion and resurrection of Jesus to be capable of bringing great good out of abundant evil. The reality of present evil and suffering is not denied, but when embraced and shot through by loving acceptance it becomes luminous and shares a resurrected quality.

Sharing the Good News

Jesus consoles, energizes and sends the disciples out to tell an unready world the Good News of universal reconciliation between human beings and God. The Christian message has radically important things to say about human happiness and fulfillment — that is what makes it Good News. The Good News is not for private consumption: it is the fire that is to be cast on the earth, to bring warmth and light. "Why do you stand looking up toward heaven?" (Acts 1:11). "Feed my lambs and sheep!" (Jn 21:15-17). Likewise, each of us in our place and time is to be an ambassador for Christ, so that the Good News is shared everywhere (2 Cor 5:20).

The community is given what it needs for its task: it must not try to "go it alone"! Jesus is Lord of the universe: he is on the shore in the Lakeside scene while Peter is all at sea, and the catch of fish comes not from human ingenuity but from obedience to the instruction of Jesus. The world is Jesus' domain — "All is given to me." There is no "secular world" from which God is excluded. God will be everywhere present, always working with us (cf. Mk 16:20; Mt 28:20).

The Holy Spirit

The Holy Spirit comes into prominence with the resurrection, empowering its witnesses to live it out in their own lives. The work of the Spirit is to enable the *koinonia* to grow. The indwelling of the Spirit means that everyone can live in friendship with God, regardless of time or place. Ours is the age of the Spirit, the eighth day of creation. A quantum leap forward has occurred in human history; the old is gone, the new is here. The good Spirit challenges the bad spirit that infects human hearts, and will ultimately prevail. Each person is the focus of the Spirit's care, and this care extends beyond death into eternal life with God.

Thanksgiving

It is right that we should "always and everywhere give God thanks and praise" (Prefaces) because of the guarantee of eternal life confirmed for us by Jesus' resurrection. "Blessed be God who has given us a new birth into a living hope through the resurrection of Jesus Christ from the dead, and into an inheritance that is imperishable, undefiled and unfading" (1 Pt 1:3-4). "Eucharist" which means thanksgiving, is used more than sixty times in the New Testament as an umbrella word to sum up the response to the Good News. Thanksgiving becomes the warp and woof of the newborn early Church. Eucharist endlessly recalls God's supreme work of love. It is not only an inner event: instead it is concretized across time and place in a meal which reveals the intimacy between the three divine Persons and us, and all they have done for us. The human members of the *koinonia* gather together with their divine friends: both groups share their stories, the vision of self-donating love is rekindled, a meal is shared, and the friendship that bonds the *koinonia* is strengthened.

Despite all that we may endure, this remembering of Jesus' death and resurrection keeps our hope steady that God is committed to having us all finally share in the family life and happiness of God. As the *Dictionary of Biblical Theology* puts it:

> In his person offered on the cross and in the Eucharist, humanity in its entirety and all the universe make a return to the Father. This wealth of the Eucharist is at the center of Christian worship.[4]

Summary

1. The resurrection of Jesus is "all about us, forever." It reveals what God thinks of us.
2. The resurrection gives a new interpretation to every aspect of our lives — our relationships, our work, our suffering and our dying.
3. In the Eucharist we celebrate what God has done and will do for us.

---

4. *Dictionary of Biblical Theology*, p. 145.

For Pondering

◊ How does the resurrection change the way you think about your own life?

◊ Can the Eucharist strengthen your sense of being in relationship with God and others?

Our Solidarity in Christ

The Poet's Eye

*I*n 1987, Margaret Thatcher, then British Prime Minister, famously stated:

> There is no such thing as society. There are individual men and women, and there are families. And no government can do anything except through people, and people must look to themselves first. It's our duty to look after ourselves and then also to look after our neighbor.

These words reflect a widespread view of human living: they have been dubbed as the epitaph for the eighties, and they run counter to much of what we have been saying about God's project for us: about the dimensions of grace and *agape* love and *koinonia*.

Is our eschatological goal an individual achievement or a corporate event? Are my fellow passengers, or those sharing the Jacuzzi with me in the gym, destined to be my companions in eternity? Is C. S. Lewis right in asserting that there are no ordinary mortals around us but only extraordinary immortals? The answers depend on the extent of our commitment to others. How much must others matter to me on a long-range basis?

If you find the argument of this chapter too taxing, at least engage with these opening lines from John Donne; note too the final reflection, which also explores the theme of human inter-relatedness:

> All mankind is of one author, and is one volume;
>
> When one man dies, one chapter is not torn out of the book, But translated into a better language;
>
> And every chapter must be so translated ... No man is an island, entire of itself ...
>
> Any man's death diminishes me, because I am involved in mankind;

> And therefore never send to know for whom the bell tolls; it
> tolls for thee.[5]

Solidarity?

Who is right, John Donne or Margaret Thatcher? Are we radically inter-related? Despite wars and rampant individualism the notion of human solidarity is not dead. The concept of the global village is renewing our awareness of inter-dependence. The Polish Trade Union which helped bring about the fall of Communism was named "Solidarity," and the world reacts in solidarity to massive disasters, as was witnessed to in 2010 when thirty-three miners were trapped underground in Chile. But many individuals live private lives and are not stirred by the notion of community: the relational doesn't catch them. Each of us is caught in some way by individualism: we are like small children who fear getting lost in a crowd. Do I *want* the final resolution of human history to include everyone, or simply the small cluster of people I'd be happy with, and of course myself? How wide is my heart?

Universal Community

What *is* God's point of view? From a divine vantage point are we one or many? The Hebrew story shows that God's ordering of history moves slowly towards solidarity. There is a broadening out from the exclusiveness of the Chosen People towards the New Testament project of a universal community. But inclusiveness demands self-displacement, and the early Christians split over the issue of including the gentiles or pagans in God's project of salvation. The little word "all" is crucial in the New Testament. St. Paul says: "As in Adam *all* died, so in Christ *all* are made alive" (1 Cor 15:21). St. John is equally clear: Jesus died not only for the Jewish people but to bring together into one body *all* the scattered people of God" (Jn 11:52, Good News version).

The yawning gap between God's ways and ours is this: God acts comprehensively, and within that, God cares for each particular person

---

5. John Donne, *Devotions Upon Emergent Occasions*, Meditation XVII, in The Works of John Donne, vol. 3. Henry Ashford, ed., London: John W. Parkes, 1839.

and thing. Creatures naturally think first about their own survival, and only slowly and with resistance do they develop wider horizons in which they consider others prior to themselves. Thus the Christian Church soon set its own limits to God's project. So there emerged the slogan: "Outside the Church there is no salvation." This distressing maxim has been superseded only in our own time by Vatican II's *Nostra aetate*, which states that all humankind has one origin and one destiny; all of us have the same origin and destiny, all are images of the one God, all are to be loved. Further, *Gaudium et spes* has restored a lost emphasis on the reality and need of solidarity. But half a century on from Vatican II, the Christian Churches avoid one another, each thinking of itself as more favored by God than the others. God's goal of all-inclusive community runs directly counter to human thinking. Here perhaps more than anywhere else we experience the truth of God's statement, "My thoughts are not your thoughts, nor are my ways your ways" (Is 55:8). The problem is not simply a historical one: we have an endemic difficulty in accepting the God-given fact that those who are "not like us" may be as much God's concern as ourselves. A breaking open of the human heart is required before we can rejoice in and support God's dream of solidarity.

Solidarity with Christ

Left to ourselves, our solidarity as a race would ultimately get us nowhere but to death. Martin Heidegger (1889–1976) emphasized that humans are beings-toward-death. But our solidarity moves into a new dimension with Jesus. Revelation tells us that we have a glorious corporate destiny beyond death. Our relationship with Christ gives us hope of glory (Col 3:4). Paul contrasts the first Adam and the last Adam: "Just as we have borne the image of the man of dust, we will also bear the image of the man of heaven" (1 Cor 15:49). The favored image for this Christian solidarity is the body: "You are the body of Christ and individually members of it" (1 Cor 12:27). The implications are startling. We have one destiny because of the Son of God who is in solidarity with us. What Christ is, we will also be. To return to poetry:

I am all at once what Christ is, | since he was what I am, and
This Jack, joke, poor potsherd, | patch, matchwood, immortal
diamond | Is immortal diamond.[6]

The divine project of solidarity — the all-inclusive *koinonia* —
is being shaped *now*, despite human reluctance and opposition, and
will be completed in the eschaton. Science, human relatedness and
theology illustrate how this happens.

Science and Solidarity

Science now takes as a given the *relatedness* of all reality. The newly
discovered history of the universe, undreamt of by previous generations, tells of our common origin some 13.7 billion years ago. Everything that is or will be in the cosmos was there in embryo when the
Big Bang took place. We share everything because we have emerged
together from the womb of the universe. With the slow development
of human consciousness, the material world began to become aware
of itself: 540,000 million years ago the first eye appeared. Some 2.5
million years ago our human ancestor, *homo habilis*, appeared on the
scene, and *homo sapiens* emerged 150,000 years ago. Less than fifty
years ago we saw pictures of the earth as a whole for the first time,
and this has immeasurably enhanced our sense that humankind
shares a common home in our "garden planet." This consciousness
has exploded via the Internet, almost like a second Big Bang. Where
before knowledge was a privilege possessed by the few, now all have
access to it. So true is this that T. L. Friedman could entitle his brief
history of the twenty-first century, *The World is Flat*.[7] His thesis is that
through Information Technology all the world's inhabitants have, at
least in principle, access to all of knowledge and its possibilities. This
has the potential to unite the race still further. Friedman recounts
his visit to a school for untouchables near Bangalore. These children,
who lived beside open sewers, said they wanted to become astronauts,
doctors, scientists, paediatricians, poets, authors, politicians. He saw

---

6. Gerard Manley Hopkins, "That Nature is a Heraclitean Fire and the Comfort of the
Resurrection," *Poems and Prose*, ed. W. H. Gardner (London: Penguin, 1953), p. 66.
7. T. L. Friedman, *The World is Flat* (New York: Farrer, Strauss and Giroux, 2005).

that they shared a global dimension of imagination and possibility with the children of the first world.

But while the accessibility of knowledge offers new horizons for solidarity and for the promotion of God's project, human progress is ambivalent because of human greed. Ronald Wright's disturbing book, *A Short History of Progress*, shows how greed is running out of options.[8] The deeper causes of our incapacity for sustained common progress are analyzed by Bernard Lonergan in *Insight: A Study of Human Understanding*.[9] The challenge for Christians is to play their part in fostering solidarity and relationships. They are to be agents of the divine solution rather than carriers of the problem.

No Distant Relations!

The thesis of the 1993 film *Six Degrees of Separation*, is that we are, at most, only six degrees of kindred away from anyone else on earth. A Microsoft analysis suggests that this may be true. Gene pools also suggest that no matter how spread out in space and time, we form a network of interconnectedness. We don't exist alone but in relationship with the life experiences of others. To know all the influences on my life you would have to know those responsible for them. Add to the mix all those whom I have or will have influenced over a lifetime, and the web spreads wider still. In short, to know me fully you would have to enter into my total life experience and that of all those around me, then of those around them and so forth. Only so could you fully understand who I am, and my place in the total scheme of things. I am indeed part of the greater self: while I am an individual, I am radically inter-connected with the totality of humankind.

All of this offers rich material for contemplation. In Rudolf Otto's book *The Idea of the Holy*, God is named as the *mysterium tremendum et fascinans* — "the mystery which is awesome and fascinating." Humankind participates in these divine qualities: we are awesome and fascinating mysteries both to ourselves and also to one another. A happy couple will say that after fifty years their partner is more a mystery to them than ever. Our grasp of the human person will

---

8.   Ronald Wright, *A Short History of Progress* (Canada: Anansi Press, 2005).

9.   Bernard Lonergan, *Insight: A Study of Human Understanding* (London: DLT, 1957).

remain incomplete until everyone's life is done. No one is insignificant. St. Paul's statement, "We do not live to ourselves, and we do not die to ourselves" (Rm 14:7), makes sense in this perspective: the life and death of each of us has an influence on others. The importance of our engaging rightly in the development of relationships thus becomes clear. For example, your good life may save another from the consequences of their wrongdoing, as when Abraham pleads successfully with God for Sodom and Gomorrah (Gen 18:22-33).

Jesus and Humankind

If each person influences all others to some degree, Jesus does so at the most profound level. When he enters into our history, everything is transformed. He is not an imposition: he comes from within, and in human form. As the Christmas liturgy puts it, "The earth buds forth a Savior." The human story now has a totally unexpected twist, as Jesus identifies with us, with our life experiences, with our living and suffering and dying. Think of history as a web which quivers with new life as each new person comes on the scene. Now imagine the web suddenly becoming brighter, more alive, in the Galilee of 2,000 years ago. It is as if a floodlight comes on, illuminating everything that was in shadow. Solidarity of a new order emerges. Through Jesus the web of humankind begins to be divinized. His irradiation of the web affects past history as well as present and future, because all history is equally present to God. The insertion of Jesus into our human solidarity in fact creates the possibility of eternal life with God. Our efforts in these pages to sketch the eschatological future of humankind have meaning only in the context of solidarity with him.

The action of the divine within the web of humanity transforms us. The sacraments convey Jesus' life to us; prayer does likewise, and so we begin to change. God works in us and we collaborate. In praying the Gospels we meet the Lord. His quickening influence transforms heart and mind, and as we catch on we become carriers of his love and grace to other members of his body. The kingdom of God advances as Jesus' values and vision radiate outwards from the Galilee of two millennia ago. Social involvement flows from this —

the work of justice, the relief of suffering, the integral liberation of humankind. The divine project of solidarity means indiscriminate inclusion even in the here and now. Thus, the eschatological community presses forward as you read these pages and try to respond to their challenge. As we have said before, the present shapes the future and the future shapes the present, so that in solidarity all can join in the great celebration that will have no end.

Helping the World

This anonymous reflection contemplates the Christian tradition of solidarity:

> What each one is interiorly, face to face with God, unknown to anyone, is of vital consequence to all; and every act of love, every act of faith and adoration, every mute uplifting of the heart, draws the whole world nearer to God.

> From each one who is in union with God there radiates a spiritual vitality, light, strength and joy which reach from end to end of the universe; a source of grace to those least worthy of it, even to those least conscious of it, and knowing nothing of how and whence it comes.

Summary

1. All humankind is in solidarity. We are interdependent – each of us affects all others.
2. To know fully one person's history will be possible only when the whole human story has been told.
3. Through Jesus a divine influence begins to transform humankind.
4. The eschatological community is taking form in the here and now, wherever inclusion prevails.

For Pondering

◊ What does the final reflection above say to you about your solidarity with others and their solidarity with you?

The Communion of Saints: a Network of Good People

History of a Truth

*T*he earlier topics dealt with — graced relationships, the *koinonia*, and our solidarity in Christ — give a new focus and energy to the truth traditionally referred to as the "Communion of Saints." This doctrine appears in Creeds from the fifth century onward. Originally it expressed the presence of grace in the Christian community, *still living in our present world.* St. Paul addresses the first Christians as "saints" (Eph 1:1 etc.). So what then were "saints"? It is hard to believe that the first Christians were much better than us. If they were different it was in their keen awareness that something wonderful had happened to them. Made holy by God's grace, they were won over by what had been done for them. Full of gratitude, these ordinary folk were living out the command of love. They were trying, even if often unsuccessfully, to be a network of grateful and altruistic people.

Then came a dissociation between Christians still living in the world and those believed to be in heaven. Preoccupation with the dark mystery of human sinfulness led to the reservation of the concept of the communion of saints to those in heaven. The canonization of exceptionally virtuous people perpetuated the gap: ordinary people felt that they didn't belong in that classification.

Welcome into the Community!

It is now time to reclaim the original dynamism of the reality of the "Communion of Saints." It is not solely a group of good people gone before us, who rest on their hard-won laurels and intercede for us who are still toiling below. Think instead of the Communion of Saints as the *koinonia* in action in the here and now — a network of ordinary good people who play their part together in God's project of building a better world.

The Network in Action

God's daring project for the world is to gather us all into the final community of love, of which the "anchor persons" are the three divine Persons. The *koinonia* is the New Testament term for those who have been caught in already, but it includes all others as *potential* members. God's project in some real way demands our collaboration if it is to succeed, and so we need to engage fully in the task. If we believe this, energy and excitement replace the boredom and dullness that can beset our lives. As we watch the ebb and flow of the human story, we can interpret it in terms of the strengthening or fragmentation of the network of humankind. We can learn to pray deeply for the world, instead of simply reacting cynically to its failures. When alerted to challenges we can ask: "What ought we do?" We begin to see our task as that of supporting a God who labors mightily with people of goodwill on behalf of the victims of our world. Each human person then becomes important to us: no one can be written out of the Great Story, because the bad as well as the good are part of the divine project. As our hearts expand, we become what we are meant to be — active members of the Network of Good People. The doctrine of the Communion of Saints then is not a dusty irrelevance but can impact on life everywhere, both in this world and in the world to come, as when we pray for those who have died.

Hints of the Real Thing

Just before writing these lines, I was on the internet, signing, with a million others from around the globe, a petition to stop the slaughter of whales. For me this was a transient but real example of how the Network of Good People can operate. You don't have to be Christian to be a member, all you need is care and compassion. The Internet is an effective way to rally the Communion of Saints! Now that local incidents of human distress can be signaled universally and immediately, the Pauline statement is truer than ever before: "If one part of the body hurts, all the other parts hurt with it" (1 Cor 12:26). Wherever people are for-one-another, the divine project is gaining ground, and the network of loving relationships — the *koi-*

nonia — is developing. Family gatherings, school reunions, parish activities, commemorations and celebrations — all are instances of networks of good people linking up. The richness in the doctrine of the Communion of Saints can be restored to Christian consciousness by indicating that it is concretized in every bonding of good people.

The New Society

The Canadian theologian, F. E. Crowe, describes this Network of Good People as "the new society of those who are God." By this he means that whereas the Father, Son and Spirit are divine by essence, we become so by participation, and so we form a society of divine and human friends. This is another perspective on the Communion of Saints. But are we divine by participation? Yes! Jesus gives us power "to become the sons and daughters of God" (Jn 1:12). Peter the fisherman is adopted into divine society and shares the nature of God — so he says himself (2 Pt 1:4). We will unfold this later in dealing with our divinization. This "becoming" is a process. The "new society" — the *koinonia* — is gaining strength by the day. We can draw courage and energy from all others who are pro-active for the good of humankind. The Network of Good People is a vital here-and-now reality, bridging the present and the future world. It holds our fragile world together, even if, as the Fox remarks to the Little Prince in de Saint-Exupéry's story, the essential is hidden from the eye.

Implications for Now

Someone has reached out a loving hand to us. We must follow suit.

"Love one another as I have loved you" (Jn 15:9). Someone in love has washed our feet: we must do likewise (Jn 13:14). Someone has died for love of us (Jn 15:13; Gal 2:20). We must be willing to do the same for others. Someone has gone to great trouble to be Good News for us, so we must become Good News to others. Christians are people who know this: we are to witness to *agape* love in our everyday lives. There are also those who know nothing of the example set us by the Son of God. Yet they live by conscience and by love, and Vatican II rightly urges us to collaborate with them. They are members of the Network. Balthasar suggests that the communion of saints is an open circle and that in principle everyone is a member.[10] The Network of Good People is not an exclusive club: it is in embryo the all-embracing Final Community of Love. Every loving activity helps to build it, and though, as of now, we celebrate only small victories and acknowledge big defeats, we hope for the ultimate victory in which each and all will be for-one-another.

Summary

1. The Communion of Saints or the Network of Good People, is focused on the transformation of present situations.
2. This Network knows no boundaries. Everyone of goodwill is potentially a member of it, because grace flows freely.
3. The Internet is an effective channel for worldwide support of those afflicted by disaster. Lively parish and local communities, together with charitable associations such as the St. Vincent de Paul Society, promote the same solidarity of care on local levels.

For Pondering

◊ Note some of the ways in which you are part of the Network of Good People, perhaps without having known it. How does this affect you?

---

10. *The von Balthasar Reader,* p. 228.

"You're Looking Divine!"

What Will Finally Happen to Us?

A friend said to me: "I like the notion that everyone's story is a graced story — that God is lovingly guiding us all along, and that God cares. But where does this graced story end? What's God's ultimate dream for us?" A good question! Does grace ultimately reach so deeply into the fibers of our being that we are transformed into the source of grace, the very being of God?

Putting this issue another way, where does human evolution stop? Bronowski's book, *The Ascent of Man*, stops at the emergence of humankind as if there was nothing further for evolution to achieve. Kegan's *The Evolving Self* leaves open the question of the limits of personal development: how far will we in fact evolve? *The Emergent Self* by van Kaam and others offers a program to deepen our love for human life and to help us realize our potential as persons. But how wide is this potential? *The Universe Story* by Swimme and Berry offers a fascinating account of the origins, development and termination of the universe, but does it leave a further story to be told? Will anything remain when our planet fizzles out?

As always, our focus will be on our divine relationships and their transforming capacity. Finding helpful terms to hint at the depth of this transformation is not easy. We are creatures who develop extraordinarily over a lifetime in body, mind, heart and spirit. But what change occurs at death? What is the next step of development, if any?

The Good News

We have seen how the Hebrews were cautious about asserting belief in the life of the world to come. It is not surprising therefore that they were silent about the nature of our future state with God. By contrast, the New Testament makes an extravagant promise about our ultimate state: we shall indeed become like God! We can speak of this only because God reveals it as our divinely intended state which begins in this life and reaches fulfillment in the next. We can humbly ask to be shown what an extraordinary promise is being made to us in the following texts:

To all who received him ... he gave power *to become children of God* (Jn 1:12)

I came that they may have life, and have it *abundantly* (Jn 10:10) Even in this world we have become *as he [Christ] is* (1 Jn 2:6). Beloved, we are God's children now: what we will be has not yet been revealed. What we do know is this: when he is revealed, *we will be like him*, for we will see him as he is (1 Jn 3:2)

He has given us ... his precious and very great promises, so that through them you ... may become *participants of the divine nature* (2 Pt 1:4)

I pray ... that you may be filled with all *the fullness of God* (Eph 3:19)

All of us, with unveiled faces, seeing the glory of the Lord as though reflected in a mirror, are being transformed *into the same image* from one degree of glory to another (2 Cor 3:18)

If anyone is in Christ, there is *a new creation:* everything old has passed away; see, everything has become new! (2 Cor 5:17)

A new *creation* is everything! (Gal 6:15)

We will all be *changed!* (1 Cor 15:51, 52)

What are we to understand from these and similar texts? What will it be like to be a daughter or son of God? How will the divine likeness show itself in us? What can it mean to be "like God" and how can we "see" God, who is Spirit?

Tradition

For help in answering these questions we turn to those who over long centuries have carried the Christian tradition. Theologians and contemplatives have pondered and prayed through the centuries over these Scriptural texts given above, and their well-considered reflections are scattered over the Breviary, the Church's official prayer book, for our prayerful assimilation.

God was made human *so that humans might become God* (St. Augustine, Brev 1:299)

Acknowledge, and now I speak with daring, that *you have been made divine* (St. Gregory Nazianzen, Brev 2:97-8)

Rouse yourself and learn to know the dignity of your nature ... If we are the temple of God and the Spirit of God dwells in us, what each of the faithful has in their souls is greater than what can be seen in the heavens (St. Leo the Great, Brev 1:511)

The faithful can say that *they are what he is*, even the son of God, even God. But he by nature, they, by sharing in his fullness, by participation (Blessed Isaac of Stella, Brev 2:597)

So — most sublime of all — *do they themselves become divine* (St. Basil the Great, Brev 2:671)

He bestowed on them *the dignity of divinity* (Basil the Great, Brev 1:447-8)

The Son of God, wishing to enable us to share in his divinity, assumed our nature, so that by becoming human *he might make us gods* (St. Thomas Aquinas, Opusc 57).

Such daring assertions could be multiplied. The Eastern Church has considerably developed this tradition of our becoming like God (*theosis*). The Western Church, however, has tended to extreme caution in unpacking the extraordinary richness of this truth, perhaps to avoid its misinterpretation. But it remains a treasure to be assimilated, and it is put before us in every Eucharist, at the Offertory: "By the mystery of this water and wine, may we come *to share in the divinity of Christ*, who humbled himself to share our humanity."

The Carthusian tradition carries the theme of *theosis*. In the film *Into Great Silence* (2005), depicting monastic life in the Grand Chartreuse in Southern France, a dramatic statement is ascribed to Jesus: "I became human for your sake. If you do not join me in becoming divine, you do me a great wrong."

Contemporary Church Teaching

Vatican II states that God's plan was to dignify humankind with *a participation in his own divine life*, and that despite sin, God still calls us to an imperishable communion of our whole nature with the divine life (*Gaudium et spes*, 2, 18). The Prefaces for Christmas and Epiphany speak of the renewal of humankind *in God's immortal image.* To be "redeemed" is not simply to be "bought back" from slavery and restored to one's former state, but to be elevated and transformed into the divine.

The *Catechism of the Catholic Church* delivers the tradition of divinization succinctly:

> The Word became flesh to make us "partakers of the divine nature" (1 Pt 2:4). "For this is why the Word became man, and the Son of God became the Son of man: so that man, by entering into communion with the Word and thus receiving divine sonship, *might become a son of God*" (St. Irenaeus). "For the Son of God became man *so that we might become God*" (St. Athanasius). "The only-begotten Son of God, wanting to make us sharers in his divinity, assumed our nature, so that he, made man, *might make men gods*" (St. Thomas Aquinas).[11]

What Can it Mean?

What can *theosis* mean? The *New Dictionary of Catholic Spirituality* says that it is the activity of the Trinity assimilating us, and the cosmos, to God.[12] Over our lifetime, we become more and more God-like, more and more similar to God in thought, will and love, in deeds and in perception of beauty. We have already noted Canadian theologian F. E. Crowe's assertion about the "new society of those who are god" which comes into being because God chooses to have us participate in divine life. We do not take on unique attributes of God, such as creation or universal providence. But since God loves us with *agape* love, our human loving becomes the same. With our hearts broken open — both through love and suffering — we come to love without limits. This is what it means to be God-like.

How Do We Become God-like?

New Age thinking asserts that we are already divine but have forgotten this truth: it sees our task to be that of growing in awareness of our innate divine status. Other religions, for example Hinduism, stress the belief that everything is already a manifestation of the divine and

---

11. *CCC*, 460.
12. *The New Dictionary of Catholic Spirituality*, ed. Michael Downey (Collegeville, Minnesota: Liturgical Press, 1993), p. 328.

that the true self is eternal. The Catholic writer, John O'Donohue, emphasizes that evangelization is not the bringing of Good News to those who do not have it, but the awakening of awareness of the divinity hidden in each person.[13] Teilhard de Chardin speaks of God's divinizing touch, which transforms both our activities and passivities — the things we do and the things that happen to us.[14]

Catholic theology emphasizes that our divinization is God's work in us. The divine and human natures are united in Jesus, the Son of God. He is already what we are to become. The Latin tradition states that we are *capax Dei*. This means that we have an unlimited capacity for God. Through the incarnation this potentiality is actualized. By assuming our human nature, Jesus releases its potential, and since he is both human and divine he stands as the paradigm or model for what human beings are to be. We have already indicated how our solidarity with Jesus implies our own divinization. The *koinonia*, which is the work of grace, implies the same outcome: love makes like, and when I am totally loved by the three divine Persons, I become like them in their loving.

The process can be seen in terms of friendship. Jesus, as we have seen, draws us into his own life through the simple yet magnificent offer of his friendship. Friends become alike, the more they share of themselves. When one of the friends is divine, the other begins to share that likeness. The Gospels indicate a recurring pattern of how people and things change at Jesus' touch: the sick are cured, demons are exorcised, the dead are raised, bread is multiplied, the storm is calmed, bread and wine are transformed to become the presence of Jesus himself. Deeper down lies another change: those who become disciples of Jesus are transformed and become progressively like their Lord.

Fully Human and Divine

He "went about doing good" — such is the laconic summary of Jesus' life in Acts 10:38, and the text adds "for God was with him." For us to be "divine" in the sense of loving with God's own love, as

13. John O'Donohue, "To Awaken the Divinity Within," *The Way*, October 1994, pp. 265–72.
14. Teilhard de Chardin, *Le Milieu Divin* (London: Collins, 1960).

revealed in Jesus, means that we become fully human. To be "fully human" from a Christian perspective is to have the mind and heart of Christ Jesus. But to develop that mind and heart over a lifetime is to become a sharer in the divine nature. We tend to imagine a strong contrast between "human" and "divine," but in Jesus these two realities are perfectly fused. Over the years we slowly become what he is from the start. More and more, the likeness of the Son is revealed in us. It is to this point that the "ascent of man" is leading, it is within this dimension that the full potentiality of the human person will flower. C. S. Lewis says that the pages of the Gospels rustle with a secret hope: he suggests that divinization may be seen as the final evolutionary step for humankind.[15]

While our divinization is God's work, it does not occur without our collaboration. God labors in every detail of our lives, opening our hearts out to love in all its dimensions. We try to respond to God, who "makes us grow in love" and to accept what comes our way unbidden, including suffering, sickness and death. Even the failures which we name as sin are brought into service for God's great project. Our growth in God-likeness will be the culmination of God's capacity to bring good from evil.

We tend to name the Holy Spirit, "the Lord and Giver of Life," as the divine Person who sanctifies, but of course all Three play their full part in it. Throughout our lives we are the focus of intense divine attention, a bit like patients who are being tended by good people — doctor, nurse and friends. Patients slip in and out of awareness of who is helping them, but this does not matter too much. The main point is that they allow themselves to be cared for, and that they pull through. The three divine Persons can be relied on to pull us through: they pull us through death into a better world.

Great heart-stretching is needed for us to "accommodate" God! The early disciples were innocent of the demands that friendship with Jesus would make of them. They had hoped for a leader who would sort out their political difficulties. Instead they are commissioned to go to the ends of the earth to preach the Good News at

---

15. C. S. Lewis, *Mere Christianity* (1941), (San Francisco: Harper Collins, 2001), Book Four.

enormous personal cost, and yet they would not have had it otherwise. Who knows what demands God may make of us, for God is indeed a demanding God. "Follow me!" and "Go into all the world!" are unambiguous commands. But all is in the service of making us like the Son, making us "divine."

What About My Son?

"How can we convey the depth of our intended transformation to a dulled world?" So asked a parent who had kindly listened to my ramblings on the matter. Since Christian belief is a one-to-one affair, I suggested, as a first step, that he try to believe it of himself and then of his two-year-old son. We talked about the fact that as a good father, he would give his son everything he could, so that the child might achieve his full potential, and that perhaps God does the same. He shyly confided that the teacher in the crèche had remarked to his wife: "You've a very exceptional child there!" We mused on just what this child is capable of. Something deeper than the physical and the intellectual? We then went on to chat about the following quotation from St. Hippolytus (170–236 AD). Neither of us understood it well, but we knew we were in the presence of blissful mystery and the father decided to turn it into a letter to his son:

Sean Patrick!

When you have learned to know the true God, you will have a body immortal and incorruptible, like your soul; you will gain the kingdom of heaven. Freed from passion, suffering and disease, you will be a companion of God and a co-heir with Christ, for you have become divine.

All that belongs to God, he has promised to give you, because you have become divine and immortal.

If you become a good follower of him who is good, You will become like him, You will be honored by him. God is not lacking in anything, and he made you also divine for his glory. Congratulations!

Your loving Dad

Summary

1. God's ultimate intention for us is that we should become like God by radiating *agape* love.

2. God works at this through everything we do and through the things that happen to us.

3. Becoming like God means becoming like Jesus in his ways of loving.

For Pondering

◊ Think of someone you love, and reflect on the fact that day by day they are in process of becoming like God. How does that make you feel about them?

◊ Can you apply to yourself the image of the patient who is being well cared for? How does it help you?

- PART THREE-

Our Journey to Fulfillment

Dying as Communion

How Shall I Die?

We move now to look at our journey to ultimate human fulfillment. We have sketched the graced relationships in which we are set, the *agape* love with which God enfolds us, and the *koinonia* or Network of Good People of which we are members. We have traced our human solidarity in Christ, and seen that Jesus through his resurrection has opened up the gates of eternal life for us. Now we take up the issue of our dying, through which we are brought to our destined glory.

Freud argued that we do not believe in our own mortality, but only in the mortality of others. To illustrate, he used a snatch of a conversation overheard in a train: "If one of us died, I would go to live in Paris!" As a priest I conduct many funeral services, but do I think of them as preludes to my own? Do I understand "for whom the bell tolls"?

The great Protestant theologian Karl Barth wrote once that on an uncertain date in the future, a group of solemn-faced men and women in sombre attire would leave the Church in which he had preached for many years and walk slowly to the graveyard. He would be among them. In the graveyard they would perform their final commendation of the deceased, and then return to the town, but without him. He would remain in the graveyard, under clay.

Why Do We Die?

The topic of death is vast: here we offer only a few ideas which may lead the reader to further personal reflection. Dying is natural to material beings such as we are. Even stars and universes die. The laws of biology operate, and revelation says that we are made from dust and so it is natural that we return to it. Death is inbuilt in us. But death in the forms in which we may experience it — as sudden tragedy, or drawn-out agony — seems outrageous. Why do we not gently leave this body behind and move to the sort of existence Jesus enjoys after his rising from the dead? Would this not have been a wonderful consequence of his saving work?

We can understand this in some way as follows. Life lies in relationships, so when a foundational relationship fails, something dies. People speak of a painful separation as a "death." The Hebrews came to link physical death, which was to them normal, with the death of the spirit, brought about by self-alienation from God. They were intensely aware of God as being the source of all life, hence "sin" or turning from God was a life-denying stance, which expressed itself outwardly in bodily death. The "fall" is understood as a radical stance of disobedience. Given the Hebrew vision of the solidarity of humankind, when the first parents turned from God in this way, all their descendants fell with them.

Granting again the solidarity of humankind with nature, they believed that our fall led to the fall of nature; nature became subject to "the bondage to decay" in some new way (see Rm 8:21).

The emergence of Jesus within the web of humankind brought a transformation of death. He was innocent and also divine, so he could die for the guilty and release them from the bondage of death. Our solidarity in sin is transcended by our solidarity in grace.

Why then does death remain? It fits with the historical unfolding of the universe. The universality of death reminds us endlessly, if we listen, of the plight of humankind insofar as it sets itself against the source of true life. Death relativizes and humbles all human achievement; it calls us to strengthen our relationship with God, to move close to the source of life and love if we are to be truly alive. We pass from death to life by loving, because "love never ends" (1 Cor 13:8). God works through the mystery of death to bring good from it, to re-orientate us to our true home. Thus death becomes a key element in saving history.

Dying as Decision for God

How then should we face death? Can we do better than Woody Allen, who quipped that he didn't mind dying — he just didn't want to be around at the time? Have we some choice about the quality of our dying? Do we die alone, or are we sustained even in our final moments by our solidarity with the web of humankind, in which the risen Jesus is central?

While animals slip away from life, dying is different for us. Although my death is inevitable, I can ignore it or prepare for it, accept it or resent it. I may or may not be conscious at the hour of my death. Dying can be sudden, violent, cruel, unexpected, dark, solitary. The sense of impending personal dissolution may bring denial, grief, fear, anger and depression before — if ever — it yields to acceptance.

Can I prepare for death now, in this time of relative tranquility? The answer is Yes. There is work I, and I alone, can do in preparing for dying. Death need not simply be the final occurrence in my life. Long before it happens, I can weave it into my relationship with God. Since my dying can be the most significant thing I ever do, let me do it well. I can choose to gather up my life and present it to God, for whom I am made. Dying can have the richness of a final, irrevocable, loving decision for God, and I can make that decision now rather than postpone it to a time when I may be unable to make it.

Throughout my life I am meant to be deciding in favor of God. Now I can gather up my life and say to God: "God, I know I am dying or will soon die. I now give myself over as totally as I can to you. Look after me and at the hour of my death take me to yourself." In my own inadequate way I can echo the decision of Jesus: "Father, into your hands I commit my spirit!" He "lays down" his life for us (Jn 10:11-17). He sees his dying as an "accomplishment" in the sense that he has completed his lifework. Our dying is enriched by having this quality: we had a mission in life, and before we die we can speak with God in relation to its completion.

While dying is something I shall endure, it is meant to be the final stage of my growth in love, my ultimate self-donation to God. But what if my life-choices have been ambiguous? I may have chosen to please myself for much of my life, rather than put God and God's concerns first, I may have made but a poor contribution to the needy of this world, but yet I also "want God."

The Fundamental Option

The concept of the "fundamental option" can help us make sense of our ambiguity. By this term is meant that there can be a radical orientation of my heart toward God, which holds me steady even though I sometimes wobble. Imagine a space craft heading for Mars: it is set, not on Venus, nor on Jupiter, but on Mars alone. While fields of stellar gravity may pull it off course occasionally, its inbuilt mechanisms correct the drift and it recovers its preset orientation. So it is with us who truly, though perhaps dimly, "want God" while wanting other things as well.

This notion of the fundamental option is consoling: it asserts that we are not at one moment in mortal sin and in the state of grace at another. Such unpredictability would trivialize God's relationship with us. We are from the outset made good through grace and set on our Godward course. While we waver on the way, sometimes seriously, repentance corrects our deviation and we move forward. We do not go back to square one when we lapse: this would equate the moral life to a celestial game of Snakes and Ladders! Of course, someone may say: "I wonder did I *ever* make a radical choice for God?" Here it is good to notice that deepest down it is God who makes a *fundamental option for us*: it is God's love and dream that sets us out on our journey. Our fundamental option, whether explicit or implicit, spectacular or hardly noticeable, is a response to God's. People who are *trying* to please God need not fear that God is critical of the quality of their lives.

The Father Draws Us

The image of the space probe hints at another powerful force which operates in our movement toward God. God is drawing us from the beginning of our journey to its end, and ceaselessly works to set up favorable conditions for us to reach our goal. Whereas the gravitational field of Mars guides the space craft home only in the final stages of its long journey, God draws me powerfully from the start, through the middle phases and at the end. This divine drawing power is stronger than any other influence in my life. While we have to believe that a person could move radically, freely and permanently away from the source of life for which they were made, the Christian community has never affirmed it of anyone. As we shall see later, the Church rightly hopes and prays that all may be saved.

Sooner or later, we may believe, the fundamental option which is perhaps hidden from us now, will be liberated. The imminence of death may bring it about. Then the pace of the drawing of God can become dramatic. As we move further into the final phase of life, we are rightly consoled by the belief that the radical love of the Son for us has already broken the absolute power of death. So while death remains as a journey through "the valley of darkness" we emerge into light, life and joy. Dying now can have a positive role: as earthly concerns diminish and self-security fails us, we can be shocked into a realization of our destiny. We leave aside secondary issues and focus on "the one thing necessary." We give in to the leading of Another. Self-concern gives way to care for others and acceptance of God. Bitterness and hardness of heart yield to quiet acceptance of people and things as they are. Kathleen Dowling Singh traces the dynamic in which dying becomes the final stage of growth.[1] God's indefatigable labor to make us grow in love finally comes to flower.

The Main Issue

Innumerable concerns face us as we come to die, but the core issue is that as human beings made for God, we can, with the help of those we love, commit ourselves radically to the relationship of love and friendship with God which has been sustaining us from the first moment of our existence. Our fundamental option thus merges into a final option for God. A healthy spirituality of living merges into a spirituality of dying, when we hand ourselves over unreservedly and become what we were always meant to be — vibrant and loving members within the final community of love.

In the context of solidarity, death can be seen as liberating, in that it is the point of our entry into the totality of human and divine relationships. This will be an extraordinary experience. The whole of

---

1. Kathleen Dowling Singh, *The Grace in Dying: How We Are Transformed Spiritually As We Die* (Dublin: New Leaf, 1999).

reality will open out before us, in all its beauty and interconnectedness. We will enter deeply into the divine consciousness, and also into the awesome wonder of relationships begun in this life. At present we can have only a few deep and satisfying relationships, and these are bordered by anxiety — a relationship may fail, and even if it survives I will die, or my beloved will die. But in the new life, the solidarity we have sketched will bring us into union with every other person, and the cosmos in all its dizzying splendor will be our playground. We need not fear, as some do, that our individuality will fade away into an undifferentiated humanity, because the divine personality of Christ will find full expression in each of us. We are already the hidden images of God, multiplied but not monotonous: then we will be radiant and glorious. There will be no boredom in the hereafter!

Hollowed Out

De Chardin speaks as follows on the transformation of death in the Christian vision:

> The great victory of the Creator and Redeemer, in the Christian vision, is to have transformed what is in itself a universal power of diminishment and extinction (i.e. death) into an essentially life-giving factor. God must, in some way or other, make room for himself, hollowing us out and emptying us, if he is finally to penetrate into us ... if the divine fire is to descend upon us ... What was by nature empty and void, a return to bits and pieces, can ... become fullness and unity in God ... The more the future opens before me like some dizzy abyss or dark tunnel, the more confident I may be... of losing myself and surrendering myself in You, of being assimilated by your body, Jesus ... Teach me to treat my death as an act of communion.[2]

Summary

1. As Christians we are called to face death as Jesus did. Thus dying has the dimension of a decision and can be an act of communion with God.
2. God works to draw us home through all the events of our lives.

---

2.   Pierre Teilhard de Chardin, *Le Milieu Divin*, pp. 69–70.

3. God chooses us "before the foundation of the world, to be holy and blameless before him in love" (Eph 1:4). That divine choice grounds our fundamental option for him, which may come into clear view only in the final phase of life.

For Pondering

◊ Do you feel you ever made a fundamental decision for God? At this stage of your life, can you hand over your future into God's hands?

The Best is Yet to Come

*T*here's the story of the little old lady who felt that her life was ebbing away. She called in the minister to make her final arrangements. "When I'm properly laid out," she said, "I want you to put a dinner fork in my hands." "Why so?" he asked. "Well, when I was young, and we'd had our dinner, my mother used to tell us: 'Keep your fork: the best is yet to come.' "

The mystery of death has been interpreted and ritualised in many different ways over the ages. Here we will sketch the central Christian tradition on death by contrasting it with other views. Christian death rituals have a quality of celebration. They are shot through with hope-filled anticipation that, despite the extinguishing of a life, the best is indeed yet to come.

- In contrast to atheists, agnostics and humanists, Christians believe in the existence of God. God, they say, is not an abstract philosophic construct but a God who cares intensely for everyone, even beyond death. The real God is "God not of the dead but of the living, for to God all people are in fact alive" (Lk 20:38). In the Christian perspective, there are no dead persons, only persons who have passed through death and are now fully alive to God and others.

- While the Greeks held that the soul survives death because of its natural immortality, Christians hold for the resurrection of the total person, body and soul. They believe that those who have died now exist in their perfected individuality, rather than simply as a memory in the mind of God.

- The central Christian belief about the transformation of death is focused on a historical person, Jesus. If it were proved that Jesus never existed, or had not risen from the dead, Christian hope in the life of the world to come would collapse. "If Christ is not risen from the dead, then of all people we are the most foolish" Paul admits (1 Cor 15:19). But this alleged event of his rising, I have argued, is sufficiently well attested to offer a mature and reasonable basis for belief that with Jesus' resurrection, death has a new meaning. "From that moment man's relation to death was changed; for the vanquishing Christ illumined for all time to come 'those who sit in the shadow of death' (Lk 1:79). He freed them from that 'law of sin and death' to which they had previously been slaves (Rm 8:2)."[3] Jesus' rising from the dead justifies our "sure and certain hope of the resurrection into eternal life" as the Anglican Book of Common Prayer puts it.

- Belief in the transformation of human death by Jesus is the key to Christian faith and hope. Christian tradition, following Hebrew thought, emphasizes the link between sin and death, but sees Jesus' saving action as achieving three things: it brings into human history the forgiveness of sin; it breaks the stranglehold of death, and it enables us to be the friends of God. Divine love encompasses sin and thereby draws "the sting of death," even though because of the distortion which sin brings into reality, we often experience death as annihilation and abandonment.

- At least since Vatican II, Catholic belief is that those who follow traditions other than Christianity or none at all are also in God's good hands, and that eternal life is accessible to all who come to mature human loving.

- Since Christ died for everyone, and since all are in fact called to the one and the same destiny, which is divine, we must hold that the Holy Spirit offers to all the possibility of being made partners, in a way known to God, in the paschal mystery.[4]

Christians are to be humbly grateful that God's Good News about the destiny of humankind has been shown to them. This news is entrusted to them for sharing: it is not a private secret. Christians, of all people, must tirelessly foster a just and inclusive society and give others hope of something yet to come, which is based on the full flowering of relationships.

Christian Pastoral Practice

We now focus on pastoral aspects of the Christian tradition about death. While we can do nothing to save ourselves from death, our

---

3. *Dictionary of Biblical Theology*, p. 118.
4. *Gaudium et spes*, n. 22.

faith opens up a vision of a world beyond. In its funeral liturgy, the Christian community magnificently expresses its belief in the saving action of God and his infinitely kind response to the prospect of human annihilation. While every death looks the same in its finality, Christians believe that something profound is going on behind the scenes. The emptiness we experience is transformed into a total openness that is filled by God.

When our time comes to die, the Christian community will gather, not simply to mourn and say farewell to us, but to see us off on our journey home to God. Jesus will be our escort of grace, to guard us on our way. He has freed us from the power of the enemy and "opened the gates of Paradise for us." He will bring us home, and is himself food for the journey, so before our human life runs out we receive the Eucharist. *Viaticum* is the old Latin term for the reception of the Eucharist when we are near death. It literally means "on the journey with you." Thus, on our way from this world to God, Jesus is our companion, another word rich in significance. "Companion" comes from the Latin (*com-panis* — "sharing bread with another"). Just as we share bread with our friends, Jesus "shared bread" with his friends, most significantly at the Last Supper, but also at the inn at Emmaus, where he took bread, said the blessing, broke the bread, and gave it to the disciples on their journey (cf. Lk 24:30). The reservation of the consecrated bread became a Christian tradition, so that if Mass were unavailable, *viaticum* would symbolize powerfully that Jesus is sharing bread with the dying person.

Jesus undertakes to save us from the forces that can destroy us: he ensures us a safe crossing into the Promised Land. The shepherd watches out for the sheep so that in our dying we may have life, and "have it abundantly" (Jn 10:1-10). God's mark of ownership is on us (cf. Eph 1:13). We like to wear brand names such as Gucci, Armani or Tommy Hilfiger, but deepest down and most precious is our Christian name, which symbolizes that God has formally named us as his own and recognizes us as such. Everyone of course belongs to God, but many do not know it through no fault of their own: we know it and are grateful for it.

Our Commendation

The Christian community entrusts the dying person to God. The act of commendation mirrors the phrase of the dying Jesus to his Father, "Into your hands I commend my spirit" (Lk 23:46). The person dying is about to embark on a journey: the Church asks God to be ready to receive her or him. Here Christian relationships come dramatically into play: the dying person remains sustained by the *koinonia* which overarches the void of death. In the moment of dying the person is still safely in the gathering of the *koinonia*, which is on this side of the void; immediately after death the person awakes to find themselves safely in the *koinonia*, on the other side. Our great fear is that dying will be like an anaesthetic from which we won't ever wake up. Awareness of the relationships that sustain us gives hope and comfort in the final stage of life. Divine and human hands are stretched out to us and will hold us tight. Love is indeed stronger than death!

A Call From Home

When you next attend a funeral liturgy, notice first the persons gathered. Most obvious is the deceased in their mortal remains, then family and friends and the wider Christian community: the presiding minister leads the intercession on their behalf. On a deeper level, Jesus is present throughout: it is he who makes Christian dying an event full of hope. He comes together with his Father and the Holy Spirit to meet the person who has died. The funeral ritual is interpersonal, the fulfilling of a loving promise — "I will come again and will take you to myself, so that where I am, there you may be also" (Jn 14:3). That promise is secure because the person who made it is divine and is totally "for" the person who has died, no matter how their life was played out.

As you attend, imagine for a few moments that this is your funeral! Imagine that the focus is on you, that it is your name that is spoken in the prayers. The key message of the readings and of the Eucharist is one of hope that Christ will bring you into eternal joy. The community will invite the Lord to remember you, and will ask the Spirit to make of you an everlasting gift to the Father. Your death will be seen as the moment when you got "a call from home" because God wants you to be with him forever. The word "home" which has so many emotional resonances, now refers to life in the company of God and of those who have supported you through life and now await your homecoming. You will not feel lonely or lost, but at home in the best of good company. Your death day becomes your birth day into eternal life.

Your body will be treated with the greatest respect, as it is signed with the Christian symbol of the cross, sprinkled with holy water and incensed. All of this is a recognition that the integral person that you were will be raised incorruptible, immortal, and glorious, body and soul. In this life you were a temple of the Holy Spirit: now the Holy Spirit, who is "the Lord and Giver of Life," will bring you totally to life.

Those who mourn you will be consoled by being reminded that "all the ties of friendship and affection which knit us as one throughout our lives do not unravel with death."[5] While you are indeed moving into a new dimension of existence with God, you will become a source of blessing for those who will miss you and who yearn to share eternal joy with you.

Symbols and Images

The image of the small boat setting sail from the crowded quayside can help. When the boat disappears from sight the shout goes up: "There she goes!" But from the other side, clear and distinct over the water, comes the cheer "Here she comes!" Early Christians used the image of a ship with a mast and pilot: the boat symbolized the Church and its captain, Christ, with his saving Cross as mast. The image recalled the disciples in the storm: by Jesus' intervention they arrive safely home (Mt 14:22-33). So will be our passing over to eternal life.

In the early Church the pagan "wake" became the Christian "vigil" or watch. The image comes from waiting through the dark night for the dawn — in the vigil, friends celebrate the dawn of eternal life for one of their number. Christian hope is that for those who have died, the best is yet to come, in contrast to the view that we simply cease to be.

---

5.   *Order of Christian Funerals* (Dublin: Veritas, 1991), p. 35.

The funeral procession has overtones of the procession of the bride to meet the bridegroom (see Mt 25:6). The Church on earth sends departing Christians on their way, and asks the Church in heaven to come to meet them. Angels and saints are asked to escort the newly arrived pilgrims to the throne of God. The grave was originally seen as a resting place on the journey to God. Flowers were sculpted on the gravestone, not just because they are beautiful in themselves, but to symbolize the Garden of Eden to which the departed person is returning. Today's funeral wreaths and bouquets have a rich and ancient meaning!

We die like beggars with empty baskets: we have nothing of our own to barter with. Our hope of eternal life depends on the generosity of God. But we believe that from the suffering and failures of life, God will bring good, and so all will be well. We can relax and let go, as with caring hands our trustworthy escort places us in the hands of a loving Father. "Do not be afraid, I go before you always!" (Dt 1:31-33). A recent book on care for the dying is called *May I Walk You Home?*[6] We can rightly imagine Jesus saying these words to us when we come to die, and the next chapter will explore the role of Jesus in the life to come.

Summary

1. Because God is good, we rightly hope that everyone may be brought through death into eternal life.
2. Christian hope of eternal life is based on the belief that the Son of God became human and broke through death on our behalf.
3. Jesus is our escort into an eternal life which is centerd on loving relationships, human and divine.

For Pondering

◊ What are your hopes and fears about dying? Can you speak with God about them, and ask for what you need?

---

6. Joyce Hutchinson and Joyce Rupp, *May I Walk You Home?* (Notre Dame, Indiana: Ave Maria Press, 1999).

Jesus at the Heart
of the World to Come

Do Relationships Endure?

"*I*'m terrified that when I die I'll find myself in a strange place where nobody knows me." Many people make remarks along this line. How can this fear be laid to rest? What continuity exists on an interpersonal level between this life and the life to come?

Some years ago I was given a seven-month sabbatical. It was sandwiched between jobs, so I took it gratefully and decided to travel, taking a month in each of seven places I had always wanted to visit. What made the experience so rich was the presence of a friend in each place. Without these friends, my various trips would have been lonely tourism.

It is likewise when we enter eternal life. We won't be alone, forming only casual acquaintances and then moving on. We will instead meet Jesus Christ, and not as a distant acquaintance. All the warmth, closeness and joy which friendship holds will be embodied in him and open to me, and he will introduce me to everyone else. Balthasar has a challenging book titled *Does Jesus Know Us? Do We Know Him?*. However doubtful we may feel in answering the second question, the reply to the first is a resounding "Yes!" He knows us through and through and loves us limitlessly. The *koinonia* — that community, fellowship, friendship or society which is divine and human and in which relationships of the deepest kind can flourish — awaits us.

Christ at the Center

All meaning in our lives as Christians comes from Christ. It is he who gathers us into friendship and opens up our relationships of grace with Father and Spirit and one another, which will reach their fulfillment at the End. He is the one who gives all he has, even life itself, for us. He is the head and we are his body. He is our brother who has gone before us, the first fruits of the rich harvest to follow.

We are inextricably united to him through the incarnation. His solidarity with us does not end with death: he does not discard us nor pass us on to someone else, his work done. Instead he is the key to our life in the world to come.

This emphasis on the risen Christ as the heart of the eschaton, present in the early Church, was lost sight of over the centuries. The focus instead was on "God," as though Christ brings the saved into his Father's presence and then fades into the background, while they enjoy the "vision of God." Vatican II has restored the emphasis on Jesus, within a trinitarian context. In the third Eucharistic Prayer, the Church prays that we may be "ready to greet Christ when he comes again" — the emphasis is on a happy encounter, a joyous homecoming to the one who wants us to be where he now is. Note the contrast with other views of death as solitary: the dead "cease to be" or they "pass on," or they "rest in peace" etc. The Christian perspective on death is unique in its emphasis on personal encounter with the risen Jesus and the other members of the Trinity.

Resurrection Scenes for Now

What can we say about this encounter with the risen Jesus? We have noted the caution of the theologian F. E. Crowe about imagining the life to come. Is silence then our only course, or has God broken the silence and disclosed to us something of how it may be?

I suggest that the resurrection scenes in the Gospels are amazingly rich, not only for our present situation as pilgrims but for our moment of arrival at journey's end. You can read and pray them as offering discreet hints which illuminate the mystery of your encounter in death with the risen Lord:

> Will he take the initiative and come to meet you as he met the women on their way from the tomb (Mt 28:9), or as he entered through locked doors to meet the disciples? (Jn 20:19)

> Will you experience him as different, yet the same, as the disciples did? (Jn 20:14; 21:4; Lk 24:16)

> Will you hear yourself called by your name, as Mary of Magdala in the garden heard her name called by a divine voice? (Jn 20:16)

Will you know him then as Mary did, and with relief fall to your knees and cling to him? (Jn 20:11-17)

Will he travel with you, as he did with the disciples on Emmaus Road and invite you to give your account of what happened over your lifetime? (Lk 24:13-24)

When you have told your story with all its hopes and disappointments, will he then "open the Scriptures" and explain everything to you, especially the hidden meaning of your sufferings, through which, surprisingly, you are entering your glory? (Lk 24:26-27)

Will your fears melt away when he says, "Peace be with you!"? (Jn 20:19)

Will he say to you as he said to the fishermen at the lakeside, "Come and have breakfast!"? (Jn 21:12)

Will he invite you to bring to him your catch, the gleanings of a lifetime — the things that you did in love, which alone will last? (Jn 21:10; 1 Cor 13)

Will he acknowledge your actions of kindness and love, and say to you, "Come, you whom my Father has blessed, take possession of the kingdom prepared for you since the foundation of the world?" (Mt 25:25-34)

Will he then take you aside as he did Peter, address you by name, and ask you simply and humbly, "Do you love me?" (Jn 21:15). And will you find yourself stammering, "Lord, you know everything: you know that I love you"? (Jn 21:17)

Will he commission you to some special role of care for those you have loved who are still in this world? (cf. Mk 16:15; Mt 28:19; Lk 24:47; Jn 20:21-23; 21:15-17)

Will you then be like the disciples, incredulous with joy and amazement, experiencing multiple overwhelmings of glad surprise? (Lk 24:41; Jn 20:20)

The God of Surprises

The Jesus we will meet in the moment of death is not someone who is indifferent to us, not a dispassionate judge. He will be, not objective, but intensely biased in our favor. The Scripture passages given above show us someone whose goodwill is total, who takes the initiative to calm our fears, who holds nothing against us, but instead is drawing us deeper into friendship and companionship with himself. This is the Lord we meet. "If God is for us, who is against us? Jesus Christ, who died, yes, who was raised, who is at the right hand of God, indeed intercedes for us. Who will separate us from the love of Christ?" (Rm 8:31-35).

When God intervenes in human history, it is always in a surprising and creative way. Scripture speaks of the "great deeds of God" which we are to store up in our hearts against our doubts. God acts mightily in creation, in the flood, in the exodus from Egypt, in the incarnation, in the resurrection of Jesus. So in our individual deaths God's intervention in Christ will be unexpected, life-giving and intensely consoling.

Summary

1. Death opens up into an encounter with the risen Lord who is on our side and loves us through and through.
2. The encounters of the risen Jesus with his disciples are characterized by his welcome, joy, appreciation. They give us hints of what is in store for ourselves.
3. God will be like the father who embraces his son, ignores his wrongdoing and welcomes him to a feast (cf. Lk 15:11-32).

For Pondering

◊ How do you envision what may be in store for you after death?

Purgatory:
Remedial Education in Loving

A Great Mistake

Some years ago I had some sessions of psychotherapy; I abandoned them only because the therapist used to fall asleep during my self-revelations. After one session on the couch, I was driving home when out of nowhere came a flash of insight: "It's all been a great mistake!" And I burst out laughing. What had been a great mistake? My perfectionism. I said out loud: "I don't have to live like that from now on. I apologize to all the people I drove mad or hurt. But from now on I will try to live more freely and more lovingly." I now refer to myself as a burnt-out perfectionist. Burn-out of course can be good! Pope Benedict notes that

> Some recent theologians are of the opinion that the fire which both burns and saves is Christ himself. The encounter with him is the decisive act of judgment. Before his gaze all falsehood melts away. This encounter with him, as it burns us, transforms and frees us, allowing us to become truly ourselves ... Love sears through us like a flame.[7]

I suggest that purgatory will be a loving and liberating experience.

Remedial Education in Loving

It makes sense that some form of purification remains to be gone through after death. The early Irish Christians thought that the very good would go straight to heaven and the very bad to hell. But they puzzled over the middle group which they termed "the not very good nor yet very bad," people with unfinished business! Most of us would see ourselves in that category. As we age, our personal "great mistake" may become clearer to us. We would wish to have been more loving, more accepting, more gracious. How then can

---

7.   *Spe salvi*, n. 47.

we come after our death to be at our best? While purgatory is not mentioned in the Creeds, Christian speculation through the ages led the Church to affirm it, most recently at Trent (1545–63).

God's project is to make us live with that special love of another kind, which enables us to love God and one another without limits. God works to "make us grow in love" throughout our lives. God sets up escorts of grace for us — parents, friends, teachers, partners. God also sets up situations that will help us to blossom: God labors too to undo unhelpful ones. God takes our pain and suffering, both physical and emotional, and crafts something wonderful from them, making us more mellow and compassionate. If this work of God is still in process when we die, it is completed through what I call "remedial education." It's *remedial* because it should have happened earlier: we weren't the best of students. It's *education* because it needs a teacher who will bring out what is present, though hidden, in us. And it's remedial education *in loving* because the lesson being taught is love.[8]

An older image of purgatory connoted a place of searing pain to which God banished us until our badness was burnt away and we were made fit for his company. It was "like an out-patients department attached to hell."[9] Now we can think of it as remedial education in loving, brought about by our encounter with Christ at the point of death. We will hardly grasp fully what is going on, but the event itself will be overwhelming Good News for us, a further revelation of *agape* love. The purification and expansion of vision and of heart will release fully our innermost potential for good. Jesus will then invite us into his family life where we will find that all are friends, both old and new. Those who meet us will say, "Heavens, what talent, what love, what goodness is there, and we hardly guessed!"

Conversion to Others

We have spoken earlier about our solidarity with one another and how we affect one another. Does our remedial education in loving

---

8. I have elaborated on God's work to "make us grow in love" in *To Grow in Love: A Spirituality of Ageing* (Dublin: Messenger Publications, 2010).

9. Eamon Duffy, *Faith of Our Fathers: Reflections on Catholic Tradition* (New York: Continuum, 2004), p. 128.

then have a communal dimension? As in the situation with which I began this chapter, will I want to apologize to those I have offended? Surely making our peace with God includes making peace with all others who are already fully with Jesus in heaven? Because they are already radiant with *agape* love, of which forgiveness is a constituent quality, asking pardon of them will not involve fear of rejection. In turn, we will forgive all those who have failed in their love for us. The process will be like the reconciliation of good friends who have run into difficulties and want nothing more than to work them through. Thus enmities and deep-seated grudges will be sorted out, and hearts will melt towards one another. Mutual forgiveness will make our relationships stronger than they could ever have been otherwise. We will elaborate on this communal dimension of education in loving when we take up the topic of General Judgment. Here let us consider this prayer of a victim of the Holocaust who died in Ravensbrück with 92,000 others:

> Lord, when you enter your glory, do not remember people of good will only.
>
> Remember those also of ill will.
>
> Do not remember their cruelty and violence. Instead, be mindful of the fruits we bore because of what they did to us.
>
> Remember the patience of some and the courage of others. Recall the camaraderie, humility, fidelity and greatness of heart which they awoke in us.
>
> When they come to judgment, grant, O Lord, that the fruits we bore may one day be their redemption.

Here we are shown another reason altogether for loving our "enemies" in the here and now. It is they who stretch our hearts the most, often to the point of tearing them open. But that pain is the occasion for making us what we are meant to be: it can bring to birth the greatness for which we are destined. There are indeed other ways, such as love, to break open the human heart, but suffering is mysteriously one of them. God copes with evil and suffering, not by eliminating them, but by bringing good out of them. So perhaps at the End we will be *grateful* to those who caused us the pain that forced us to grow in love. Surely in death we will meet our "enemies" and talk things through with them, perhaps consoling them and enabling them to forgive themselves for the things they may have done to us?

Gospel Insights

In the Gospels a succession of people encounter Jesus individually and, to their surprise, their lives are changed. Their unexpected meeting with him changes their lives beyond their hopes and dreams. I suggest that our encounter with Jesus in death will likewise be transformative of us.

The lakeside encounter (Jn 21) provides an image of how things may be. The disciples are cold, tired, hopeless and empty-handed. A figure appears on the shore in the grey dawn who tells them where to fish and they suddenly land a great catch. Out of their misery comes joy. Instinctively, John, the beloved disciple, recognizes the mysterious figure and cries out: "It is the Lord!" In death, when we are cold, empty, and without hope, will we, to our amazement, find that Jesus is already alert to our situation and is coming to the rescue?

When Jesus has met the disciples' immediate needs he initiates an intimate dialogue with Peter. The agenda is clear: it's all about love! Jesus searches Peter's heart: Peter's past failure underlies the conversation, but is dealt with so delicately! Jesus' approach is positive, not critical. "Do you love me?" is the all-important question, asked three times, surely with a wry smile. Peter is drawn out of himself into total trust: "Lord, you know everything; you know I love you." No need for an act of contrition: his statement of love is enough to indicate his change of heart. How did he relate from then on with his companions? Turned inside out, disconcerted, but humbly grateful to find his friendship with Jesus so simply restored, he surely from then on saw all relationships differently.

This scene offers us an image of our unique personal encounter with the risen Lord in death. The focus will be on Jesus, not on myself. A shattering event it may be indeed, one that breaks my heart open. But because it is enfolded in limitless love and understanding, I will be able to bear it. I will see my life from a divine perspective. As

Peter was examined in love, I will be likewise. The truth that "love is all that matters" was available to me during my life but somehow I often lost sight of it. I will see that my self-centered style of living was a great mistake. Will I have regrets? Surely, but they will be integrated into my new history. The memory of my failings will only help to highlight the dazzling awareness that "the Mighty One has done great things for me, and holy is his name" (Lk 1:49).

There will be a joyous quality to all this. The prodigal son's return made the father's heart leap for joy, and Jesus rejoiced when Peter finally said "Yes, Lord, I love you." There is joy also among the members of the *koinonia* in heaven when a person finally sees the light. Our remedial education will bring a joyous sense of completion to ourselves, for we will have become what we were meant to be from the first. We will then have truly passed "from death to life."

Particular Judgment

We have been talking all along about what is called "particular judgment" in contrast to "General Judgment." Particular judgment highlights an important reality: that each person is unique, not simply part of the collectivity. I am responsible for myself. As an image of particular judgment, think of two friends. The first has all the qualities one could ask of a good friend. The other is less than dependable and has an addiction which leads to serious lapses. So the relationship runs into difficulties. The good friend thinks things through and sets up a meeting with her struggling friend, who at first dreads the encounter but finds to his happy surprise that love and forgiveness prevail. In this atmosphere, he admits to his failings and repents of the hurt and damage he has caused. But more than that, he finds himself moved to the depth of his being by the quality of love she shows. The root of the addiction is healed, and he becomes truly free for the first time.

Particular judgment in the past was seen as a fearful future event, a reading of the ledger of our lives as in a court of law where justice must take its course. But we do not need God to show us the imbalance between credits and debits, because faced with *agape* love we will know interiorly how sadly short we have fallen. Instead, particular judgment will be a creative and healing moment. We are held, loved limitlessly and invited into new life. Our sins are not held against us, though the damage they have done to others and ourselves must be healed.

The doctrine of particular judgment advises us that as far as possible our encounters with others should be creative moments, which bring energy, joy and freedom. We must try to act towards others now as mercifully as we ourselves would wish to be met then by the Lord. God holds no grudges, nor must we. We are invited to act now out of the *agape* love which already embraces us: this would transform the atmosphere around us and bring joy to God.

Prayer for Those Who Have Died

> Where the prayers for the dead in the early Church were mostly petitions for rest, light and peace … the memorial prayers of the Middle Ages were mostly cast as prayers for the release of suffering.[10]

Purgatory was imagined as a busy and thronged center of correction, so such prayer became a major task for monasteries. And it was lucrative too, so it led also to aberrations in regard to indulgences, all of which the Reformers swept away. Yet prayer for those who have died is effective because of the fellowship that links this world with the next. The *koinonia* or fellowship revealed in the New Testament transcends space and time, and if one part of the body hurts, the others hurt with it and should come to assist it (see 1 Cor 12:26). The effects of prayer are free from the limits of time, because prayer is set in the divine dimension. So I can pray effectively today for someone who died years ago. As Pope Benedict says:

> In the communion of souls simple terrestrial time is superseded. It is never too late to touch the heart of another, nor is it ever in vain … Our hope is always essentially hope for others.[11]

---

10. Eamon Duffy, *Faith of our Fathers*, p. 127.
11. *Spe salvi*, n. 48.

Help From Those Already in Glory

Those who have reached their full development strengthen the *koinonia*, and so we are helped by them. They are no further from us than God is, and like God they are engaged in helping us. They cheer us as we make our way along our pilgrim path. They were once like us, so they know how to help us. They are "for us" — on our side — and give us hope of the ultimate victory of love. They see what we do not yet see, so they intercede for us and help us through the unseen rhythms of grace. No one therefore is completely alone and isolated. To quote Balthasar again:

The communion of saints ... in the widest sense is the community of all those for whom God on the cross has suffered total abandonment. *And that indeed includes everyone.*[12]

There are few more consoling doctrines when we are worrying about those who have died than that of the *koinonia* or Communion of Saints.

Summary

1. Purgatory is not a process of punishment but of healing, a transformative meeting with the risen Lord in which the frozen areas of our hearts melt through encountering pure love.
2. Many Gospel scenes shed comforting light on the quality of our final encounter with the risen Jesus.
3. Our present and unending struggles to accommodate the inadequacies of others are part of our current remedial education in loving. Our compassion must gradually extend to all who have not yet reached their divine destiny.

For Pondering

◊ "In the evening of life you will be examined in love" (St. John of the Cross). How is your preparation for that test coming along?

---

12. *The von Balthasar Reader,* p. 329.

- PART FOUR -

Could Things Go Horribly Wrong?

Judgment as Reconciliation

An old aunt of mine, who had spent all her life in West Cork, was persuaded once to come to Dublin, and she stayed with us. One evening my parents brought her and myself to the "pictures." At about 10.30 p.m. she stood in the city center watching the cinemagoers flood onto the street, and exclaimed: "My God, what will it be like at the General Judgment?" Hers was a problem of logistics, but to most of us, the logistics of the event would be the least of our worries on the last day!

History of the Concept

We have already looked at what is called "particular judgment." Part of our encounter in death with the risen Lord will be a personal and unique review of life against the backdrop of *agape* love. Scholars debate whether there is also need of a general judgment. What, after all, would it add to particular judgment? The New Testament has differing attitudes to the issue: St. Luke speaks only of particular judgments — as in the parable of the rich man and Lazarus (16:19-31); or Jesus' last promise: "Today you will be with me in paradise" (23:43). Matthew emphasizes only universal judgment (25:31-46) and his heart-rending scenario has captured popular imagination ever since and eclipsed other versions of this great mystery. St. John's insight is that a favorable judgment of humankind has taken place already — "God so loved the world that he gave his only Son, so that everyone who believes in him may not perish but have eternal life" (3:16). This means that the stance we take regarding Jesus will be *ipso facto* our "judgment." In all this ambiguity about the precise nature of judgment, the core truth to which we must adhere is given in the fifth-century Creeds: Jesus Christ will come "to judge the living and the dead."

General judgment on the world's inhabitants is a central scriptural theme from the flood onward. A simple image underlies it: the king returns to his domain and judges his subjects. So on the "Day of the Lord" God will come in power, and his justice will triumph: Faithful subjects will be vindicated, while the evil will be punished. Hence the Judgment scene in St. Matthew, in which Christ will be the Judge and will divide humankind as a shepherd divides sheep and goats. The criterion for salvation in this account will be openness to the needs of others.

But here, General Judgment is simply a repetition, only now in public view, of all particular judgments. There is no reference to a judgment of the corporate personality of humankind, no sense of solidarity. I propose instead that general and particular judgment balance one another. Particular judgment indicates that we are not simply part of the collectivity: what we do matters eternally, while General Judgment emphasizes that humankind is a unity and that ours is a corporate destiny. I will say more on this below.

Church Teaching Today

The statements of Jesus regarding hell are now to be understood as dramatic exhortations to conversion while there is still time.[1] This is a welcome shift of interpretation. The focus of this conversion remains as indicated in Matthew 25 — conversion is toward my needy neighbor. This endorsement by the Magisterium of recent biblical scholarship and theological insight contextualizes many scriptural texts which seemed to assert the certainty of eternal loss for many.

> The affirmations of Sacred Scripture and the teachings of the Church on the subject of hell are a call to the responsibility incumbent upon man to make use of his freedom in view of his eternal destiny. They are at the same time an urgent call to conversion.[2]

Again:

> The message of the Last Judgment calls people to conversion while God is still giving them "the acceptable time ... the day of salvation." It inspires a holy fear of God and commits them to the justice of the Kingdom of God.[3]

---

1. *CCC*, 1036, 1041.
2. *CCC*, 1036.
3. *CCC*, 1041.

The reality of our solidarity in Christ, already outlined, suggests indeed a General Judgment, but understood in a new way. Eschatological events are interconnected, as we stated at the beginning: they do not stand alone. The reality of Christian relationships, the *koinonia*, the breadth of *agape* love, the hope of universal salvation, the project of God to bring all humankind into the final community of love — such truths must contextualize the doctrine known in Christian tradition as "General Judgment." The following points can be made:

- We may hope that General Judgment will be favorable to all. Why? Because the judge is Jesus Christ, who is one of us, rather than over against us as judge against accused. Human history has been transformed by the incarnation. God's decision in favor of the world is a "general judgment" already: God is on our side: we have been acquitted of our wrongdoing (Rm 8:31-39), so our task is to live out this reality in the here and now.

- General Judgment, understood as God's decisive action in human history, will be creative and life giving, as are all God's interventions. God labors for the salvation of all humankind, to ensure a joyous final outcome of history.

- Since eschatological truths are to illuminate present praxis, General Judgment highlights the corporate destiny of the race and the importance of corporate decisions.[4] It calls us to despair of no one but instead to labor for the rehabilitation of those who are excluded or who exclude themselves.

Who Will Judge Whom?

Granting the solidarity of the human race and our solidarity with Christ, who is "one of us," the question arises: who will judge whom? This is where the traditional term of "judgment" is inadequate. Judgment by one person of another or of a group is an adversarial matter. But our premise is that relationships always remain central in the *koinonia*: where there is breakdown, they must laboriously be restored. Again, solidarity means instead that those who adversely affect the group of which they are part must be reconciled with it. What each

---

4. For more on the role of Christians at meetings, see Brian Grogan and Phyllis Brady, *Meetings Matter!: Spirituality and Skills for Meetings* (Dublin: Veritas, 2010).

of us does or fails to do affects all the other members of the human family, because our lives make up one single story. Sin is the enemy of solidarity, of good relationships and of the divine project.

We are subjected to and in turn radiate negative influences. What we call "personal sin" not only damages the individual: it wounds the greater self, that conscious and reflective body of humanity of which the sinner is part. To amend, the individual must ask pardon of all, and forgiveness must be given freely by all. This radically alters the notion of judgment.

Family Reconciliation

To follow through on the above, let us for a moment set aside the image of judgment and think instead of family reconciliation. Recall the happy family sketched out in the chapter on graced relationships. The parents and the son have invited everyone in: guests can stay as long as they like. They become adopted into the family and share its happiness. Now imagine that divisions emerge: some members quarrel and become alienated, while others bring discredit to the family name. The original family ponder what to do, and decide eventually that only a full scale reunion will bring about reconciliation. Because they love everyone, they work hard to soften each heart towards the others. They try to maximize the prospects of reconciliation.

When the reunion takes place, everyone is asked to give an honest version of how they stand in regard to the others. Behind the scenes, the family works to help people understand who their enemies might be, and to emphasize the bonds that people have with one another despite their differences. They remind the hard of heart that the person whom they hate is "the brother or sister for whom Christ died" (Rm 14:15; 1 Cor 8:11). Wrongs on all sides are acknowledged. Each is asked if they can forgive, knowing that in turn they will have to ask forgiveness themselves: "Forgive, and you will be forgiven" (Lk 6:37). Reconciliation comes at its own price and its own pace: enmities are slowly put aside.

Does this seem bizarre, or does it link in with what goes on in ordinary life? We spend our lives negotiating relationships — the

New Testament is full of advice on how to do this well. It seems strange to think that all this might end with death.

We have said earlier that the divine viewpoint is comprehensive: God thinks of humankind in a global fashion as well as individually. God is not small-minded! The term "Chosen People" referred to every member of the Hebrew nation, the bad as well as the good. Those who were trying to escape from Egypt were not filtered out according to merit when crossing the Red Sea. Likewise, all of us are, from God's point of view, members of the *koinonia*. We are in solidarity with one another and with Christ, whether we know it or intend it or not. Therefore, that God should plan not only particular reconciliation but a general reconciliation of humankind is at least imaginable.

A friend of mine was going away for a few days to a wedding, leaving her husband and three children to manage for themselves for the first time. Having seen them off in the morning, she worked hard before heading off herself: she filled the freezer and the fridge with good things and anticipated their individual preferences. When the family came in the first evening they found the table beautifully set, and a note between the pepper and salt canisters. It read: "While I'm away, don't be horrible to one another, because I love all of you!" When she came back, she knew at a glance that something had gone amiss. She cried a bit, then sat them down and said: "Let's sort this out together!" And they did. And while it would be an exaggeration to say that they lived happily ever after, substantially they have done so, and they still have her note stuck on the door of the fridge. The God of the New Testament is revealed as a reconciling God, who does not hold our wrongdoing against us (cf. 2 Cor 5:19). God remains so in the world to come.

Summary

1. The Church has indicated that statements about hell are to be understood as dramatic calls to conversion to others.
2. Since Christ is in solidarity with us, "judgment" need not be seen as adversarial and punitive, but as a creative restoration of flawed relationships.

3. Family reconciliation can offer a rich image of what judgment may be like.

For Pondering

◊ What does the notion of family reconciliation suggest to you in relation to general judgment?

How Far Will God Go For Us?

We shall deal here with two issues: firstly, the statement in the Creed that Jesus "descended into hell" and, secondly, the discredited theory that unbaptized children would never see the face of God.

Jesus Among the Dead

In its efforts to catch on to the full implications of Jesus' resurrection, the early Church was led to consider the ultimate fate of those who had already died. Believing that Jesus' death and resurrection were meant to be Good News for all humankind, they thought of those who had already died and constructed the image of him descending into the world of the dead and bringing out those imprisoned there. So St. Peter says:

> He was put to death in the flesh, but made alive in the spirit, in which also he went and made a proclamation to *the spirits in prison*, who in former times did not obey. (1 Pt 3:18-19)

The Church's liturgy has long set aside Holy Saturday to enable the believing community to ponder this mysterious aspect of Jesus' redemptive work. We acknowledge, as we must, both the saving intention of God and the real possibility of its rejection. We have to live humbly with the contradictions involved in portraying a divine event which overarches human categories of space and time. Speculative theology suggests the following points:

1. The descent of Jesus to the realm of the dead is a saving event of God. The redemption won on the Cross is asserted as working out across space and time, and even within the unpromising domain of the dead. Faith affirms against all the odds that no one may be thought of as being beyond the reach of *agape* love. St. Thomas Aquinas makes the point that even the damned (if there be such) are still the focus of God's love.

2. Jesus is pictured as being in total solidarity with sinners. He has died, as sinners do, and now he endures the consequence

of sin at the outermost bounds of existence where life is no more, where human beings despair of rescue, where all relationships fall apart and communication is impossible. But the solidarity of Jesus with humankind remains still; God's hand is not withdrawn.

3. As the "firstborn from the dead" Jesus proclaims eternal life to the dead. He establishes limits to the power of evil and death, for "he has the keys of Death and of Hades" (Rev 1:18). He is the first fruits of redemption: the harvest follows. The reality of this divine activity in the underworld is highlighted by this image of descent into "hell." "Blessed be the Lord, the God of Israel! He has visited his people and redeemed them" (Lk 1:68, Grail Version).

4. Early Christian writers were divided on whether the "harrowing of hell" by Jesus released everyone or only the good. The harrowing is magnificently described in "An ancient homily for Holy Saturday."[5] The solidarity of Jesus with his brothers and sisters "who sit in darkness and in the shadow of death" is portrayed thus: "Rise, let us go hence; for you in me and I in you, together we are one undivided person."

While the Church warns against the theory of apokatasasis, according to which the eternally damned — including demons — are restored to God, the mystery of the descent into "hell" is invoked to affirm the saving work of God even after death. The doctrine of purgatory acknowledges this post-mortem saving action. Balthasar and Karl Rahner have speculated on its universality.[6]

Limbo

This twelfth-century theory about the eternal borderline status of the unbaptized gained unwarranted theological status when presented as fact by pastorally insensitive preachers and catechists. It was never part of the *sensus fidelium*, because Catholic parents were

---

5. Brev 1:320–2.

6. See J. R. Sachs, "Current Eschatology: Universal Salvation & the Problem of Hell," *Theological Studies*, 1989, pp. 227–54, and Hans Urs von Balthasar, *Dare We Hope That All May Be Saved?* (San Francisco: Ignatius Press, 1986).

torn between wanting to be with God in heaven and wanting to be with their excluded child.

Only with Vatican II was belief expressed in the power of God to achieve the salvation of all.[7] Where previously, unbaptized children received neither funeral service nor burial in consecrated ground, the Roman Missal now includes a liturgy for them.

The *Catechism of the Catholic Church* does not use the term "limbo" and takes a long-overdue pastoral approach:

> As regards children who have died without Baptism, the Church can only entrust them to the mercy of God, as she does in her funeral rites for them. Indeed the great mercy of God who desires that all men be saved, and Jesus' tenderness toward children which caused him to say: "Let the children come to me, do not hinder them" allow us to hope that there is a way of salvation for children who have died without Baptism.[8]

Given the developing sensitivity to the non-Christian world, and also to the ever-increasing number of abortions, Pope John Paul II asked the International Theological Commission to study the question of limbo. In April 2007 that Commission issued a forty-one-page statement on *The Hope of Salvation for Infants Who Die Without Being Baptized*. Limbo, it said, reflects an unduly restrictive view of salvation:

> People find it increasingly difficult to accept that God is merciful and just if he excludes infants, who have no personal sins, from eternal happiness, whether they are Christian or not. The number of non-baptized infants has grown considerably, and therefore the reflection on the possibility of their salvation has grown more urgent. There are theological and liturgical reasons to hope that infants who die without Baptism may be saved and brought into eternal happiness, even if there is not an explicit teaching on this question in revelation.

So we may close this sad chapter in Catholic theology, while learning its unintended lessons.

Firstly, we do not have to understand *how* God may bring about the salvation either of those who die in serious sin, or of the non-baptized, or indeed of anyone else, including ourselves! With God

---

7.   See *Nostra aetate,* and also *Lumen gentium,* n. 16.
8.   *CCC,* 1261.

everything is possible. Since God desires everyone to be saved (1 Tim 2:4) we may believe that the dynamics of Christian relationships carry beyond death, and who can set limits to them?

Secondly, it is not the task of theology to force God to submit to Scripture texts poorly interpreted. Further, *theory and speculation* should be acknowledged as such, and theology itself must become a *collaborative* work of the People of God: married and female scholars must be included. A theologically literate parent would not countenance the theory that an all-loving God could consign their child to limbo. Unbaptized children are de facto within the *koinonia* as are all of goodwill: those not of goodwill are also included, but one-sidedly as yet.

Summary

1. The statement in the Creeds "he descended into hell" means that Jesus entered into redemptive solidarity with all humankind, including sinners who have died.
2. God is working to achieve the salvation of all, and with God, all things are possible.
3. The parable of the lost sheep (Lk 15:3-7) makes us cautious about setting limits as to how far God will go in search of us.

For Pondering

◊ "God's hand is never withdrawn." How does that statement affect you in regard to your own life?

Will All Be Saved?

The focus of this book so far has been to prepare the ground for responding to the question: "Will all be saved?" What solid grounds exist for the Christian hope that God, despite our worst efforts, can bring about the salvation of all humankind? The sordid evidence of much of human history seems to point to a negative response, but thoughtful minds may help to make us think afresh:

- St. Augustine asserts that even sin can be accommodated in God's plans.

- "God writes straight with crooked lines" (Portuguese proverb).

- When Aslan the Lion in C.S. Lewis' *Chronicles of Narnia* is asked why he dealt harshly with one of the children, he responds: "No one is told any story but their own!"[9]

- Paul Claudel, in his introduction to *The Satin Slipper*, says "All things minister to a Divine Purpose and so to one another... Even the falterings of circumstance and the patternings of personality, sin and falsehood, are made to serve truth and justice, and above all, salvation in the long run."[10]

- "Catholic tradition would seem to speak with a very faltering voice on the victory of good over the power of evil. On the whole, it has been haunted from the time of Augustine with the fear of hell."[11]

Such comments could be multiplied. We enter on this topic aware that "now we see in a mirror, dimly" (1 Cor 13:12). We do not know the final outcome of anyone's life, no matter how distorted it may have been. We are ignorant, but what the medievals termed "learned ignorance" (*docta ignorantia*) is better than none. So we proceed humbly in the light of the revelation that is given us.

---

9. C. S. Lewis, *The Horse and His Boy* (London: HarperCollins, 2009), p. 217.
10. Paul Claudel, *The Satin Slipper* (London: Sheed & Ward, 1931), pp. vi–xi.
11. W. Dalton, "The Wages of Sin," *The Way*, July 1975, p. 193.

In Tune With God

One dull morning a few years ago, I was lying in bed debating with myself about getting up. Unbidden, the idea came to me: "What gets God up in the morning is the saving of the human race!" That thought, at least on occasion, motivates me to rise to face the day.

That God intends to save all is clearer in Church teaching than ever before. Vatican II states:

> Since Christ died for *everyone*, and since *all* are in fact called to one and the same destiny, which is divine, we must hold that the Holy Spirit offers to all the possibility of being made partakers, in a way known to God, in the paschal mystery.[12]

But will God succeed? Or perhaps the saying is closer to the truth which says, "God is alive and well, but working on a less ambitious project!" How true is it to say that the future belongs to God, given our human capacity to wreck even the best of plans? Whether all will be saved will be revealed only at the close of history. But I need to ask: would I honestly want the salvation of everyone — that neighbor from hell, that domineering cleric, that corrupt politician, those financial swindlers, those terrorists and torturers, or those guilty of crimes against humanity? If my honest answer is "No!" I need then to ask, as a Christian, "Does God view these people as I do, or through some different lens?"

Human Thinking

Two contrasting traditions exist about the fate of all humankind: the first is born of human thinking. Most of us would say that the world's blatant injustices should be reversed, at least at the end of time. Such was the Jewish mind in the time of Jesus: the Hebrews looked forward to the Day of the Lord, which would see them vindicated against their oppressors. We tend of course to presume that *we* will be on the right side when things are finally sorted out. We judge ourselves by our intentions, but others by their actions. One of my community used to humbly acknowledge his faults, and then add a few lines beginning with "But to be fair to myself ..." I don't

---

12. *Gaudium et spes*, n. 22.

recollect him saying that of someone else's misdemeanor. Are we like the Pharisee in the Temple who despised the sinful but repentant publican at the back? (cf. Lk 18:9-14). From Jesus' comment we know that from the divine point of view he had got it all wrong. What makes us think that we will be saved, but that others may be lost? Do we really want justice for ourselves, rather than mercy? Which of us could stand before God at the end and say: "Lord, I have lived out the Gospel and I'm now claiming my inheritance"? We need to be wary of thinking in human categories!

Divine Thinking

Divine thinking runs differently to ours (cf. Is 55:8-9). Jesus rebukes Peter at one point and accuses him of thinking *in human terms* (cf. Mk 8:33). In the Emmaus story, Jesus turns inside out the minds of the two disciples by his reinterpretation of his passion. He calls them "foolish" and says "Was it not right that the Messiah should suffer these things and then enter into his glory?" (Lk 24:26). Two thousand years on we still struggle over that divine assertion about the positive aspect that can be revealed in human suffering. Again, Jesus confronts his parents as a child: "Did you not know? ... But they did not understand" (Lk 2:49). He scatters the orderly logic of the religious leaders in his effort to get them to accept a God whose approach to the oppressed and broken is totally different from theirs. Divine thinking is hard to take on board. It's less a matter of our coming to *understand* God's thinking than humbly accepting it. St. Paul admits: "How unsearchable are God's judgments and how inscrutable his ways!" (Rm 11:33). He is saying: "We know the divine project, but we can't see how God will get there. Divine thinking is much too profound for us and our minds are so small. But God will see this project through."

Divine thinking expresses divine loving, which is limitless. God will go to any lengths to achieve his loving purposes in us. We know the extremes to which a good parent will go in order to help an "impossible" daughter or son. "I'd go to hell for the sake of my son" a woman once said to me. Thus, while evil can leave *us* powerless, it moves God to effective and often dramatic action. God is not fazed by human malice but instead works endlessly to bring good out of it, as is shown in the passion. The love of God has a terrifying quality in its intensity, as the whisky priest admits in Graham Greene's *The Power and the Glory*:

> It would be enough to scare us — God's love. It set fire to a bush in the desert, didn't it, and smashed open graves and set the dead walking in the dark. O, a man like me would run a mile to get away if he felt that love around.[13]

Divine Resources

Our resources to cope with problems are very limited, but God's are limitless. I can't control the weather, nor my height, nor my life span, nor my ageing, nor can I easily stop even children from doing their own thing! The dimensions of our lives over which we have little or no choice are far more numerous than those within our freedom. God is different! As the ultimate source of all that exists, God can cope. Nothing falls outside the scope of divine providence. The Trinity embraces us all. "We live within the circle of the Trinity. No one or no thing can fall outside this circle," as John O'Donohue puts it.[14] God orchestrates everything, even the bad vibrations and toxicity emerging from warped human freedom.

God is directly responsible for all that is good, as the liturgy reminds us, and wrestles with what is bad to bring good out of it. God touches wayward minds and hearts to desire the truth and love for which they were made. God accepts our bad choices, but does not then step back and passively leave us to their dire consequences. Instead God reconfigures our situation to put us on the right path again. If one divine intervention fails, another is devised. God has privileged access to our hearts and minds — not surprisingly, since he made us. God is indefatigably focused on the task of our salvation, though it will take "all the time in the world" to bring it to completion. The three divine Persons are "on the job" with their limitless resources, while respecting our freedom and our sensitivities. We might all carry notices saying: "Caution — God at work!"

---

13. Graham Greene, *The Power and the Glory* (London: Vintage, 2010), p. 197.
14. John O'Donohue, "The Priestliness of the Human Heart," *The Way Supplement* 83, 1995, p. 47.

And so we must dare to hope and work for the salvation of all. As long as we desire the damnation of "the wicked" — that is, those other than us! — we frustrate God. God desires the opposite, and needs us to help in the efforts to save all. In ways that we need not fully understand, our efforts to live rightly influence the outcome of human history.

Why Bother Being Good?

Many people would like to believe in the possibility of universal salvation. But then they ask, "Well, if we're all going to be saved, why bother being good? Being bad would make life a lot easier!" A few responses can be given. The argument in this book is that universal salvation is a legitimate hope, but not a divine guarantee. We must not take it for granted! Next, "being saved" does not mean that we can scrape into the cosmic party by straightening a tie or adjusting a hairstyle at the door. We are invited into nothing less than becoming truly sons and daughters of God. Membership of the divine community awaits us, and it calls for radical interior change so that we become like God (see Mt 5:48). In this life our task already is to become members of the Network of Good People of whom Jesus is the pivotal figure. We are therefore to grow steadily in *agape* love, to make this world a better place in which the *koinonia* can flourish. In its atmosphere, the world becomes a good and safe place for people to achieve their full potential, and also for nature to flourish in all its delicate beauty. Eschatology cannot be divorced from present concerns. With these clarifications we turn to look at the evidence supporting the possibility of the salvation of all.

Support from Scripture

There are some two hundred references in the Scriptures to the reality of hell: it suffices to quote the best known: "You that are accursed, depart from me into the eternal fire prepared for the devils and his angels" (Mt 25:41). These dramatic words have possessed the Christian heart and imagination since they were first spoken, and led to the obvious conclusion that humankind will finally be divided into blessed and damned. As we have noted, this division appeals — at least at first glance — to our human ways of thinking.

There is however another set of texts, less well known, which refer to universal salvation: they offer a key insight into the mind of God on our topic:

> This is the Lamb of God who takes away the sin of the world (Jn 1:29)

> I will draw all people to myself (Jn 12:32)

> It is not the will of your Father that one of these little ones be lost (Mt 18:14)

> If God is for us, who is against us? It is God who justifies. Who is to condemn? (Rm 8:32-34)

> God desires everyone to be saved (1 Tim 2:4)

> The wedding hall was filled with guests, both good and bad (cf. Mt 22:10).

Other texts asserting God's intentions to achieve universal salvation include John 5:21; Romans 5:18-20 and 11:32; 1 Corinthians 15:20-28; 2 Corinthians 5:19; Ephesians 1:10; Colossians 1:20; 1 Timothy 1:15 and Titus 2:9. The term "all" recurs over and over again in reference to the effect of the saving entry of God into our history. A primary text is Romans 9–11: the argument in this daring passage is that the disbelief of the Jews has become the occasion for the gentiles to receive the Gospel: but this in turn will arouse the Jews to repent and return, and so all will be saved. Thus, what initially appears to be a failure of the divine plan results in the salvation of all. "The gifts and the calling of God are irrevocable … God has imprisoned *all* in disobedience so that he may be merciful to *all*" (Rm 11:29-32).

Support from Tradition

Henri de Lubac's *Catholicism: A Study of Dogma in Relation to the Corporate Destiny of Mankind* shows that among the early Fathers of the Church there was a consistent belief in the social nature of salvation. "The whole of humankind makes one image of God."[15] For Tertullian, the Church is Catholic or universal "in depth" and in this way includes

---

15. Henri de Lubac, *Catholicism: A Study of Dogma in Relation to the Corporate Destiny of Mankind* (London: Burns & Oates, 1950), p. 211.

everyone.[16] For Methodius, the Church is in the pains of childbirth until all people shall have entered into her.[17] Claudel, echoing the Fathers of the Church, says that sinners, "deprived of daylight, worship in the night."[18] St. Irenaeus says: "By the wood of the Cross the work of the Son of God was made manifest to all: his hands are stretched out to gather all people together."[19]

Support from Church Teaching

Since it is the case that two conflicting traditions about universal salvation co-exist, we turn to the Church's teaching on what we should believe and how we should act.

"The souls of those who die in mortal sin descend into hell" — such has always been the unambiguous teaching of the Church.[20] But note that the Church has never taught that anyone is in hell, and in Vatican II there is a repeated hope that all will be saved. We read in *Gaudium et spes*:

> The form of this world, distorted by sin, is passing away, and we are taught that God is preparing a new dwelling and a new earth in which righteousness dwells, whose happiness will fill and surpass all the desires of peace arising in human hearts. Then death will have been conquered, the daughters and sons of God will be raised in Christ ... When we have spread on earth human dignity, communion and freedom ... we will find them once again, cleansed this time from the stain of sin, illuminated and transfigured, when Christ presents to his Father an eternal and universal kingdom ... Here on earth the kingdom is mysteriously present; when the Lord comes, it will enter into its perfection. The Church has but one sole purpose — that the kingdom of God may come and that the salvation of the human race may be accomplished ... The Word of God ... was made flesh, so that as a perfect man he could save all women and men and sum up all things in himself.[21]

---

16. Ibid., p. 18.
17. Ibid., p. 123.
18. Ibid., p. 191.
19. Ibid., p. 207.
20. See *CCC*, 1035, 1056.
21. *Gaudium et spes*, n. 39, n. 45.

While some theologians simply assert that all will be saved, the Church here expresses hope, not certainty. But how do we reconcile this hope with the bald assertion that those who die in mortal sin go to hell? We have already quoted the new *Catechism*:

> The affirmations of Sacred Scripture and the teachings of the Church on the subject of hell are a call to the responsibility incumbent upon man to make use of his freedom in view of his eternal destiny. They are at the same time an urgent call to conversion.[22]

Again, the message of the Last Judgment calls people to conversion while God is still giving them "the acceptable time ... the day of salvation." It inspires a holy fear of God and commits them to the justice of the Kingdom of God.[23]

Thus texts speaking of damnation are to be interpreted not as previews or advance notices of a disastrous end for some persons, but as *warnings* of what will happen if we are not converted — converted, that is, to one another, because what we do to others we do to the Lord (see Mt 25:40, 45 and Acts 9:5).

But let's not let go of the older tradition without pushing it to the limit. Surely it is true that many die in mortal sin and therefore are in hell? Again however, contemporary Church teaching cautions us:

> Mortal sin is a radical possibility of human freedom, as is love itself ... Our freedom has the power to make choices for ever, with no turning back. However, although we can judge that an act is in itself a grave offence, *we must entrust judgment of persons to the justice and mercy of God.*[24]

For the Christian community, the salvation of all is thus an open possibility. A contemporary theologian, J. R. Sachs, summarizes current Catholic eschatology as follows:

- Because we are free, we can reject God

- Hell would be self-chosen final alienation from God, not a place of sadistic punishment instituted by a vengeful divinity

- Neither Scripture nor Church teaching affirm the final loss of anyone

---

22. *CCC*, 1036.
23. *CCC*, 1041.
24. Ibid., 1861.

- Salvation and loss are on contrasting planes of possibility because all God's labor is to save humankind
- Certainty about final judgment is impossible, but because of Christ's victory over sin and death, we may and must hope that all will be saved.[25]

Favorable Judgment

We noted earlier that God has already passed favorable judgment on the world: "God so loved the world ..." (Jn 3:16). "If God acquits, who is to condemn?" (Rm 8:33-34). "In Christ, God was reconciling the world to himself, not counting their trespasses against them" (2 Cor 5:19). God, who is faithful, will not reverse that judgment at the end. Judgment has been given in favor of the accused.

Our hope for the favor of God is set in the solidarity of Jesus with us, which we have explored above. He is one of us and on our side, not against us as a judge. He thinks of each of us as a sister or brother for whom he died (see Rm 14:15; 1 Cor 8:11). Since his destiny is glorious, we can hope that ours will be too. The interconnectedness of all is such that the history of any one person involves the history of all. The human story, of which Jesus is the hero, is a single epic of cosmic dimension, in which the harrowing of hell is a central moment. We noted too that the General Judgment will not be simply a "freezing" of the facts of our lives, a rubber stamping of our final balance sheet. We do not need God to show us that we are "in the red." Rather we may hope that final judgment will be — as are all God's actions in our lives — creative, life-giving, surprising, extravagant, truly Good News. Finally we suggested that the image of family reconciliation might serve well to illuminate the process by which the "ministry of reconciliation" might be achieved (2 Cor 5:18-20).

Nothing Too Tough for God

The hope of universal salvation, treasured in the early Church, gradually gave way to pessimism. Yet Christian tradition has always treasured a deep hope that all may be saved. Despite massive evil,

---

25. See J. R. Sachs, "Current Eschatology: Universal Salvation & the Problem of Hell," *Theological Studies*, 1989, pp. 227–54.

Christian prayer and liturgy has always expressed the hope that God's kingdom may come, that our trespasses may be forgiven, that God's saving will may be achieved. The contemplative tradition too has held to the hope of universal salvation. Monks and nuns intercede for the whole world. In his encyclical on hope, Pope Benedict endorses a medieval statement: "The human race lives thanks to a few; were it not for them, the world would perish."[26]

Finally, there is the recurring emphasis in Scripture that God can do what we cannot achieve. This theme first appears when the aged Sarah's pregnancy is announced: "Is anything too wonderful for the Lord?" (Gen 18:14). Her husband Abraham was also convinced "that God was able to do what he had promised" (Rm 4:21). The humbled Job admits that God can do all things, and that no purpose of his can be thwarted (Job 42:2). Jeremiah says simply, "Nothing is too hard for you" (Jer 32:17). The theme is echoed in the New Testament: Jesus will be born of a virgin because "nothing will be impossible with God" (Lk 1:37). And when asked, "Who can be saved?" Jesus says "For mortals it is impossible, but for God all things are possible" (Mt 19:26 and Mk 10:27; Lk 18:27). It is as if God takes delight in doing "the impossible"!

Dare we then hope? Yes, we must be in harmony with the Church, which takes its cue from revelation, in hoping that all be saved. Further, this hope must liberate energy in us to work, to pray and to make sacrifices for the salvation of all, not excluding ourselves.

Arguments of the Heart

How could I be eternally happy if someone I love were damned? More importantly, how could God be happy, since he loves us all with *agape* love and could not bear the loss of anyone?

Our generation has a unique understanding of the psychological complexities which limit human freedom: thus we can better distinguish subjective from objective wrongdoing.

---

26. *Spe salvi*, n. 15.

Are there any personalities so devoid of goodness that an infinitely loving eye can find no grain of compassion in them? And if such exist, is the fault their own or rather that of others?

While some sinners may not want their own salvation, they remain in solidarity with the body of humankind, among which Jesus is the central figure. May this be enough to save them? Arguments in favor of universal salvation depend not on our goodness but on God's. God is greater than our hearts, and they need to be enlarged so that our concerns match those of God. More will be said on this issue in the next chapter when we deal with hell.

Summary

1. Old Testament hope for the punishment of the wicked, so natural to human thinking, has survived into the New Testament, and still flourishes today.
2. The official reinterpretation of texts which speak of damnation eases the way to accommodating those texts which hint at universal salvation. "Sinners deprived of daylight, worship in the night."
3. Like Julian of Norwich we may hope that "all will be well."

For Pondering

◊ "Nuke them all: let Allah sort them out!" was a popular car sticker after 9/11. How do you feel about that?

Might Hell be Empty?

"Not Without My Brother"

Some years ago a Dublin family decided that they would bring a child home from the local orphanage for Christmas day. When the father arrived a little girl was sitting waiting for him. "Are you all set?" he asked. "No" she said fiercely, "I won't come without my little brother!" So he negotiated that and the pair had a great day. The family loved them so much that they adopted both, and they are now living happy lives. The girl's words echo those of Jesus spoken long ago: "Father, I want those you have given me to be where I am" (Jn 17:24). And surely the Father's response is the same as that of the father of the family.

We have already dealt with critical issues in regard to hell when considering the question of universal salvation. Although so great a scholar as Newman believed that most people would go to hell "like a herd of swine, falling headlong down the steep" we must approach the issue, not from the point of view of individual sinners, but from the massive foundation of Christian relationships.[27] Since the incarnation, no one can be understood apart from their relationship with Jesus. However weak that relationship may be from the human side, its strength comes from the divine side where Jesus is. Further, human solidarity within which Jesus is the central influence is such that it becomes difficult to conceive how an individual could break away from every relationship. Even the worst of tyrants, such as Hitler, still have someone who loves them and sees the spark of goodness in them, which lies below their worst excesses. In his *Conjectures of a Guilty Bystander,* Thomas Merton speaks of the divine point in our depths which is beyond sin and alienation: it is only at God's disposition, not ours. Tyrants are eternally in a divine relationship, though their human relationships may be disastrously negative.

---

27. See Eamon Duffy, *Faith of Our Fathers,* p. 134.

Here we will consider three points: Christian tradition about hell, whether anyone is totally evil, and whether hell may be empty. While hell's imagery is to be abandoned, we must retain the core value in Jesus' warnings about eternal loss. The possibility of ultimate human failure emphasizes that present living is critically important and that our gifts and energies must be committed to building a more just and inclusive society (cf. Mt 25:31-46). There can be no trivializing this challenge: nothing can substitute for radical conversion to our neighbor in their need. Hell shows what we are capable of. It is not an act of divine but of human sadism. It is revealed as an intra-worldly, freely chosen phenomenon in Auschwitz, Hiroshima, the Gulag, Uganda, in the crucified peoples of Latin America. There is a dark side to us, whether we name it as original sin or otherwise, something that makes us close our hearts to one another and our better selves. But the perpetrators of evil are also our brothers or sisters "for whom Christ died" (Rm 14:15, 20; 1 Cor 8:11), so our hearts must be stretched to accommodate them, else we thwart God's project of the universal community of love.

Christian Tradition

All religions have to deal with the issue of life after death, and consequent reward and punishment. In earlier Old Testament thought, all the dead, drained of life, were gathered in Sheol. Later, in light of the fact that the good suffer and the wicked prosper, justice suggested that the good rest in God, while the wicked are punished (Wis 4:19, c. 150 BC). Gehenna, a burning refuse pit outside Jerusalem, provided the background for New Testament images of fire and worms, darkness, weeping, grinding of teeth, torments, thirst (cf. Mt 3:12; 13:50; 22:13). St. Paul speaks of eternal pain but uses less imagery: the wicked are banished from the face of God (Rm 9:22; Phil 3:19). For St. John, those who disobey the Son will not see life, but must endure God's wrath (Jn 3:36).

Hell is named in the Creeds from the fifth century on, but only in reference to Christ's descent there, interpreted as limbo, where the just were awaiting release. Jesus "will come to judge the living and the dead" — there is no mention of the division of good and wicked. The Creeds conclude with belief in the forgiveness of sins, the resurrection of the body, and life everlasting.

The theory of the redemption of the damned and of demons was condemned by the Council of Constantinople (543). Various Councils, including Trent, assert that there will be eternal punishment immediately after death for those who die in mortal sin. Punishment will be proportionate to sins: punishment of the senses and the spiritual torment of loss of God are distinguished. It is inferred that the damned may suffer in their bodies even before the Last Day. Vatican II is silent on hell, but the Vatican letter on *Certain Questions Concerning Eschatology* (1979), restates the Church's belief in its reality. The new *Catechism*, as we have seen, offers a fresh and compassionate interpretation of texts which previously were taken literally to infer a final division of humankind into saved and lost. Further, the *Catechism* tells us not to judge anyone: "Although we can judge that an act is in itself a grave offence, we must entrust judgment of persons to the justice and mercy of God."[28]

Totally Evil?

Hell would be the eternal state resulting from the final choice to be a non-relational being. Such a closed attitude to others would set a person in contradiction with the relational dynamic of the universe established by God. The remark attributed to God that "it is not good for humans to be alone" (cf. Gen 2:18) would be fully verified in the utter aloneness of the lost in their eternal restlessness.

We have to ask: does such a person exist? Is anyone totally evil? But we must ask from God's point of view, not ours. God is *for* sinners: this is what *agape* love is about. All the influences, bad and good, that human solidarity bring to bear on a person are known to God. God's hand remains stretched out towards them in friendship and is never withdrawn. The full resources of divine love, energy, imagination and commitment are focused on winning them over. We can set up in our minds a totally depraved person and ask what will happen to them if they do not change; but we could only know the

---

28. *CCC*, 1861.

actuality of this scenario if it were revealed to us: we cannot project from possibility to actuality. It may be that a tyrant is mad and thus to some degree be non-responsible.

An international court can condemn to death someone guilty of crimes against humanity, but in another world there is no condemnation, only pardon: "It is God who justifies. Who is to condemn?" (Rm 8:33-34). The issue is not whether God or others will forgive, because forgiveness is a given in the divine domain. The issue is whether the sinner can accept forgiving love. Perhaps only in death will hardened sinners know fully the truth of things about themselves, others and God (cf. 1 Cor 13:12), and this knowledge may bring them release from self-alienation and rejection of others. Perhaps they have never known what it is to be human. Studies show how the relational dimension of the brain can remain undeveloped, so that the person afflicted emerges as intelligent but primitive and inhuman. Lionel Shriver's *We Need to Talk About Kevin* portrays, through his mother's eyes, an "impossible child" who executes a number of his schoolmates.[29] The critical absence of healthy relationships is highlighted here.

Might Hell Be Empty?

We have noted earlier Balthasar's speculation about the descent of Jesus to hell to win sinners over, not by power but by helpless love. One of his books is titled *Dare We Hope That All May Be Saved?*[30]

Further, he notes that since the middle ages a steady line of female witnesses have kept alive Christian hope for the salvation of all. They include Julian of Norwich, with her confidence that all will be well. She speaks of the as yet unknown deed that the Trinity will perform on the last day, "through which deed he will make all things well."[31]

St. Thérèse of Lisieux expresses limitless hope for the salvation of everyone. Saint Edith Stein argues that there are no limits to grace,

29. Lionel Shriver, *We Need to Talk About Kevin* (London: Serpent's Tail, 2006).

30. Hans Urs von Balthasar, *Dare We Hope that All May Be Saved?* (San Francisco: Ignatius Press, 1986). Balthasar's arguments for the salvation of all have been criticized severely, if not always fairly. See, for example, John Finnis, *Religion and Public Reasons* (Oxford: Oxford University Press, 2011), chapter twenty-four, "Hell and Hope."

31. Julian of Norwich, *Showings,* long text (New York: Paulist Press, 1982), chapter 32.

and goes on: "Human freedom can be neither broken nor neutralized by divine freedom, but it may very well be, so to speak, outwitted."[32]

These women, going against the male logic of their times, have expressed their belief that somehow — God alone knows how — all may be saved. They believe, as they must, in the possibility of hell, but they also believe, as they may lawfully do, that hell is empty. They are not to be dismissed out of hand: Thérèse is a Doctor of the Church, and Edith Stein a Patron of Europe.

To add a male voice to this chorus, de Chardin asserts that sinners are always under the influence of Christ, and that it will be difficult for them to resist endlessly the power of love which sweeps through the universe. Despite evil there is also an inexhaustible treasure in each individual. His consolation is this: "You have told me, O God, to believe in hell. But you have forbidden me to hold with absolute certainty that any human being has been damned."[33]

Making Life Hell

In Sartre's play, *No Exit*, three characters arrive in hell to discover that they have to spend a sleepless eternity together in a small room. After a while, one says, "Hell is other people" — meaning that other people make life hell for us if they diminish us. Positive affirmation and recognition are basic human needs: others shape our lives to a large extent and assign us our identities. Maya Angelou describes how she found herself poor, black, young and female during the Great Depression, and the great struggle she had to exist as a person. Such scenarios, in New Testament terms, create the kingdom of Satan. The kingdom of God has the opposite dynamic: as we have noted from Walter Wink, in God's world there is no domination: everyone is "for" everyone else. Any action that works against this creates "hell." If hell exists, it is we who create it by relating badly.

We must then foster just and loving relationships, no matter how demanding the task and how unpromising the outcome may appear. To the Rabbi who decides to abandon his bad flock, God thunders: "Go back to my people, for I have sunk myself in them!" In our time,

---

32. Quoted by Balthasar in *Dare We Hope That All May Be Saved?*, pp. 219–21.
33. De Chardin, *Milieu Divin* (London: Collins, 1960), p. 141.

we have the instance of the South African Truth and Reconciliation process, which attempted to rekindle healthy relationships in the face of appalling brutalities.

Summary

1. To set your heart against another is to be on the borderlands of hell.
2. Gospel texts on hell are not previews of a final division of humankind into saved and lost, but dramatic warnings to include others in our concerns.
3. Christian hope liberates energy and love for the task of ensuring that no one will be missing at the End.

For Pondering

◊ Recall a struggle you have had to forgive someone who betrayed or hurt you deeply.
◊ What does non-affirmation do to your sense of yourself? Do you work hard to encourage others in their struggle for their own identity?

- PART FIVE -

Fulfillment

"Are We There Yet?": Time and Eternity

For Ever and Ever?

We use the terms "eternal" and "eternity" constantly. To be a Christian, we have said, is to be focused toward eternal life, where we will be members of the final community of love. But what does "eternal" mean? If you were asked to speak for one minute about "eternity" how would you fare? Eternity is hard to grapple with and not easy to define. We can't avoid employing the word "time" but then we have to say, "It's the opposite of time."

Let's ask a wise man named Boethius for help! He lived in Rome, was orphaned at seven, became one of the most learned men of his day, held high positions in the state, but in 524 AD was unjustly executed for treason. During his turbulent life he wrote *The Consolation of Philosophy*, in which he says that eternity is "the simultaneously whole and perfect possession of unending life." If that seems hard to grasp, think of people about whom you say, "They've got it all together!" Think then of unfortunate people about whom we say, "Their lives are falling apart!" For us human beings, life keeps changing. But God's life is truly all together, always. It is NOW.

Because we get bored easily, we can imagine eternal life as boring, "an endless Holy Hour." Adrienne von Speyr (1902–67), a Swiss convert, wife, medical doctor, author, mystic and colleague of Balthasar, has a comment about boredom. Before the fall, she says, everything was fresh and original; but after it, boredom and predictability set in. This image illuminates the idea that boredom is peculiar to our time-bound world but not to the realm of the eternal.

People who are fully alive are neither bored nor boring, and in the world to come, everyone will be fully alive. The three divine Persons will be Life Itself, like a fountain always pouring itself out. Eternity is all about life *to the full* (Jn 10:10).

We say of a dramatic moment, "It seemed like an eternity" meaning that time stood still. Eternity, however, is not just static or endless time: it is closer than we think, and vibrant with life. It is as near to us as God, and God is already all around us. "In him we live and move and have our being" (Acts 17:28). "The Eternal" can in fact be another name for God, since it is a uniquely divine quality. God dwells in a dimension other than ours, bounded neither by time or space. That world would be totally inaccessible to us unless God had kindly invited us into it, but by being gathered into the *koinonia*, into relationship with God, we are brought into the eternal.

Eternity, therefore, is now no longer remote: it encompasses time, because the divine embraces the human. Eternity is calling us home to itself. Children ask "Are we there yet?" Clearly we are not yet fully there! But we are partly so: a few considerations will indicate the immediacy of the eternal to us.

Prayer

When you kneel down at your bedside to pray, or take time out for a graced moment in the middle of a busy day, you are already breathing the air of the eternal. In the simple Morning Offering we time-bound travelers link our days with the eternal. Any advance in our knowledge and love of Jesus, Son of God, is a step forward into the eternal domain, a movement "from here to eternity," to borrow the title of the 1953 classic film. Hence the value of cultivating contemplative moments, in which we "take a long loving look at the real" and see the world and ourselves as God does.

Christian Living

In the biblical view, God created all reality, and "it was good." Humans too were "good" and in relationship with God, who walked companionably with them in the Garden. At those privileged times, the eternal and the temporal met in harmony. When sin spoiled our relationship with God, the "eternal" became a distant world: we lost the experience and harmony of the divine. God then seemed to be removed to another world. Now, however, the Church with its sacramental life, especially Word and Eucharist, becomes the new gates of eternal life. Whereas in the Genesis story, the gates of Eden were closed and defended against human incursion, they are now open to all, so that we can be "at home again" with God.[1]

The Eternal Embraces Us

John O'Donohue says that "behind the veneer of our external lives the eternal is at work ... It is quietly creative."[2] The NOW of God is already here. It sustains and underpins our temporal world, like the deep unmoving root of a great tree. Time, then, is already in the divine, eternal dimension. The eternal is not in the future: it is more present to us than time itself, because it is "just here," whereas time is passing.

Further, humankind is being eternalized by the presence among us of the Eternal One. The incarnation places our story within the eternal. St. John's Gospel emphasizes that we already have a foretaste of eternal life through relationship with Jesus (6:47). The eternal is now, even though — because we are time-bound — we feel that we have only a precarious grasp of it: or better, that it has only a precarious grasp of us! So "Are we there yet?" can be answered affirmatively, even if only conditionally.

Building Eternity

We saw earlier how cautious F. E. Crowe is in imagining life after death. Yet here he speaks of eternity in a startling and accessible way:

> ... my every action has its eternal aspect. Every idle word and every passing thought become part of the granite mountains of the universe of being; they do not vanish into the past but remain and are in eternity. If we must use the language of time ... the familiar expression that "our good works go before us" that they are sent ahead and stored up for our "future" is closer to the truth than the view that they simply vanish into the past ... With every moment we are building eternal reality, adding another brick to our house of being. In daily converse we try to forgive and forget, but the universe of being cannot forget.[3]

1. Adrienne von Speyr, *The Gates of Eternal Life* (San Francisco: Ignatius Press, 1983).
2. John O'Donohue, "The Priestliness of the Human Heart," *The Way Supplement* 83, 1995, p. 43.
3. F. E. Crowe, *Lonergan and the Level of Our Time*, p. 375.

"You're born: you suffer: you die. End of story!" But is it so? In Crowe's view, what we do carries into eternity and is critical in shaping the final arrangement of things. Everything done, good or bad, has a permanent connotation, though in "the new heavens and earth" only what is irradiated by love will endure. This concept is expanded on by de Chardin in *Le Milieu Divin*, in regard to the divinization of our activities and our passivities.

The Authentic Present

At the end of his scholarly study of Catholicism, French Jesuit Henri de Lubac says the following:

> The hereafter is far nearer than what we call the present. It is the Eternal found at the heart of all temporal development which gives it life and direction. It is the authentic present, without which the present is like the dust that slips through our hands.[4]

The Supreme Moment

Pope Benedict XVI has this to say about eternal life:

> Eternity is not an unending succession of days in the calendar, But something more like the supreme moment of satisfaction, in which totality embraces us and we embrace totality.
>
> It would be like plunging into the ocean of infinite love,
>
> A moment in which time — the before and after — no longer exists. We can only attempt to grasp the idea
>
> That such a moment is life in the full sense
>
> A plunging ever anew into the vastness of being, In which we are simply overwhelmed with joy.[5]

---

4. Henri de Lubac, *Catholicism: A Study of Dogma in Relation to the Corporate Destiny of Mankind* (London: Burns & Oates, 1950), p. 201.

5. *Spe salvi*, n. 12.

Summary

1. God's life is all together always, it is NOW. Eternity is life to the full and it awaits us.
2. Time is underpinned and sustained by the eternal. We are already "in" eternal life.
3. We are building eternity in all that we do.

For Pondering

◊ My every action leaves its imprint on eternity. How does this idea sit with you?

Heaven: the Ever-Flowing Celebration

*I*n the "good old days" when Irish Jesuit students were numerous, we used have an annual fortnight's holiday by the sea. Money was scarce, so scope for individual recreational preferences was heavily curtailed. The whole operation was known as "Organized Joy." Once, in the early sixties, we got news that a small-town hotel had been located for us, ten miles from a beach on which a corpse had recently been washed up. Dismayed, we decided to make the best of it, all of us, that is, except one who begged the Superior, "Please don't send me there: if I'm allowed to stay here I won't cause trouble. I'll read and look after myself." His passionate request was refused.

For some people even the limited fun attached to present living outweighs the doubtful fun to be hoped for in the world to come. Few of us want to die. To most of us, heaven seems to be nothing special, as Rahner has noted. Is it "organized joy" or an extended solemn choir practice on a dull Sunday afternoon? Or is it, as this book implies, all about relationships of the most enjoyable kind? Is it like a gathering of good friends who find happiness in one another's company, are fully free and creative, and have no fear that they will have to be tidy, servile or demure? "To be human is to be an immense longing," according to Rahner. Will that immense longing be satisfied? One of my colleagues who was terminally ill with cancer believed so: he put at the end of all his emails: "Working for God doesn't pay much, but the retirement plan is out of this world."

As a simple outline scheme for a vast topic we will consider heaven under three aspects: God, Meaning, Joy. Scriptural references will be given, to satisfy doubting hearts.

God

God is a gifting God, and heaven is God's final and endlessly generous gift, the happiness of the family life of the three divine Persons.

We will enter into their unfathomable joy (see Mt 25:21, 23). The great promise of the New Testament will be fulfilled; "In the world to come, eternal life" (Mt 19:29). All is given out of love: it does not depend on merit, and it has no demands attached; "All that is mine is yours" (Lk 15:31). God is the indiscriminate and lavish host of the banquet.

"The lover gives all to the beloved" is St. Ignatius' description of God blessing us even in this world. This is what grace means: the concrete love of God for us, life in abundance. But "Grace is glory in exile, and glory is grace at home," as Newman says. While grace is in exile here below, it has a hard time of it, and we often doubt its capacity to overcome the disgrace with which we litter the human story. God's only resource is love, and that seems pitifully inadequate against the strength of evil.[6] But when grace is at home, we will see its glory.

Grace is all about good relationships, solidarity, friendship, the bonding of the *koinonia*, the network of good people. Each of us will be for-one-another, as the three divine Persons are for-one-another-and-for-us. We will find ourselves appreciated, admired, rejoiced over, totally accepted, delighted in, important. Each will be an honored guest at the wedding feast (Mt 22:1-10); the morning star will rise in our hearts (cf. 2 Pt 1:19), and we will be "revealed in glory" (Col 3:4). We will be first-born citizens (Heb 12:23) with all the freedom that this implies.

We Shall See God

In popular thinking, the focus in the world to come can turn spontaneously to human relationships at the expense of our relationship with God. But God is our future, it is for God that we are made. Traditionally, the term "beatific vision" has been used to emphasize that we shall meet God "face to face." The Curè d'Ars preached a famous three-sentence homily: "When we go to heaven, we shall see God! We shall see God! We shall see God!" He could say no more but wept.

---

6. See Balthasar's *Love Alone: The Way of Revelation* (London: Burns & Oates, 1968).

Since God is pure spirit, what can it mean "to see God"? How do the three divine Persons "see" one another? Our seeing of another whom we love is a humble mode of relating: it draws us deeper.

"Seeing" and "vision" in relation to God are umbrella terms to cover the inexpressible experience of *direct relationship* with the divine. We shall know God in a qualitatively new way: we shall enter into the mind and heart of God as never before. Faith will yield to personal knowledge. We will understand then that God is truly "in all his words most wonderful/most sure in all his ways." We will "see" the plans of God as having been plans for peace and not disaster, to give us a future and a hope (cf. Jer 29:11). Most importantly, we will understand how God worked in our suffering and brought out of it good that would never have existed otherwise.

Shortly before his death in 1984, Karl Rahner wrote the following reflection:

> Within that immense terror that is death will come a cry of unutterable joy which will reveal that the immense and silent void we experience as death is in reality filled with the primordial mystery we call God. It is filled with God's pure light, with God's all-absorbing and all-fulfilling love.
>
> Perhaps in this incomprehensible mystery we can catch a glimpse of Jesus, the Blessed One who appears to us and looks at us. It is in this concrete figure of Jesus that all our legitimate assumptions about the incomprehensibility of the infinite God are divinely surpassed.[7]

The beatific vision will be ours. "Now we see in a mirror dimly, but then we will see face to face. Now I know only in part: then I will know fully, even as I have been fully known" (1 Cor 13:12). We who have lived in the dark night and in the cloud of unknowing will move into clear luminous vision. God will smile on us, as God has always done: we shall see that smile on the face of Jesus. The phrase, "You gazed on me and you smiled," which summed up the life-experience of a seventeenth-century French mystic, will be fulfilled for all and each of us.

---

7. *The Cambridge Companion to Karl Rahner,* eds. Declan Marmion and Mary Hines (Cambridge: Cambridge University Press, 2005), pp. 309–10.

How Love Changes Everything

The Three-Personed Love which is God will transfuse everything and everyone. Love will be seen to have conquered, against all the odds. We will see love's radiance in everything: no loving deed or desire or prayer of ours is wasted, but will come to full flower. "We will reap at harvest time" (Gal 6:9). All that was not love will fall away, but love will remain because it is eternal (1 Cor 13:8).

We will have endless joy in allowing God to be his loving Self for us unreservedly. In this life, we fear that God may not be wholly for our good, but then we will know otherwise. What mystics experience in flashes of the touch of God, we will experience then in limitless abundance. We will then become boundless love — for God, for each other, for ourselves and for all creation. Consider Julian of Norwich's words:

> I was taught that love is our Lord's meaning. And I saw very certainly in this and in everything that before God made us, he loved us, which love was never abated and never will be. And in this love he has done all his works, and in this love he has made all things profitable to us, and in this love our life is everlasting.[8]

God's *agape* love will be fully free to play in everything: this self-displacing servant love will bring endless joy to us weary pilgrims.

Praise

We applaud those who carry out difficult feats. Rudolph Nureyev, the Russian ballet dancer, once received over eighty ovations at the end of an inspired performance. Praise of God can be weak in us in this life because we do not understand God's action well. But when all are safely gathered in, the authors of the epic of human history will step onto the stage: there will then be endless praise for each of them and for all together. Our ovation for God's achievement will flow endlessly and fill the cosmos.

The particular wonder of each of the divine Persons in the Trinity, and how marvelously they relate, will be a source of our unending wonder and praise. We will never tire of God: there will always be

---

8. Julian of Norwich, *Showings,* ed. Edmund Colledge and James Walsh (New York: Paulist Press, 1978), p. 86.

more to appreciate: we will be brought from one glory to another, as Gregory of Nyssa says. The wonders of God's providence will become clear to us, and we will marvel that truly everything has been turned to good, in ways we could never have imagined. All things will be seen as interconnected within themselves and with God.

Meaning

The Meaning in the Story

Only at the end, when the last person is gathered in, will our search for meaning be satisfied. In the meantime we puzzle endlessly, asking "What's the meaning of this?" Is it all, as Macbeth puts it, "a tale full of sound and fury, signifying nothing"? No! Meaning, divine meaning, will emerge, as through the incredibly tangled set of events we call human history, God brings about the Final Community of Love. This was God's purpose all along: it will now be revealed as having won through despite the disasters of sin, malice, and death, which here below wreck community. The odds seemed impossible, but with God all is possible.

We will share our stories. The mysterious interconnections in the narratives will endlessly amaze us. We will marvel together at the goodness and wisdom of divine providence in shaping the Great Story. There will be the joy of discovery that everything fits in. There will be tears of joy at the recovery of what we thought was wasted effort and unanswered prayer. The Body of Christ (1 Cor 12:12-27) will now be complete in all its members, and we will see the part we played in its growth, and how even our wrongdoing was the occasion of good for those we injured.

Forgiveness and reconciliation are central in Jesus' teaching. I have suggested that final judgment may be seen in terms of a family reconciliation, so that in the final community there will be no barriers or antagonisms. With wounds healed and hatred eliminated, we will radiate compassion, sympathy, kindness and mutual understanding. Each of us will know that we are fully safe in the company of the others. In this life, my neighbor's inadequacies impact on me, sometimes dreadfully: yet that same person is a potential manifestation of the perfection of God. At the End, that image will have been perfected.

The Meaning of Suffering

We talk a great deal in this life about suffering. What meaning will we find in it in the next? Here we gather up some of the principles which help to contextualize it.

- "When I can see I can cope!" So a friend often says to me. But often we cannot see why bad things happen to good people. At the End, however, we will see the comprehensive nature of God's planning. In ordering everything, God orders each event: within universal divine providence God cares for the individual. Only within the final all-embracing view will we see how our present troubles find meaning. We will accept that while the resurrection of Jesus and the establishment of the *koinonia* were God's radical historical response to evil and pain, their final resolution had to await the close of the human story, because the life of each affects all.

- The Law of the Cross (*Lex crucis*) — better named "The Graced Dynamic of Suffering" — will be seen then to have borne its fruit. The outcome of the passion reveals to us that unavoidable suffering, patiently endured, plays a vital role in the world's redemption. At the End, the discordant notes of our suffering and endurance will have been integrated into the completed symphony of human history.

- Often we simply endure in darkness; often we obstruct God's dream. We will see that it is the characteristic of God to bring good out of what is bad, and that God, while respecting our wayward freedom, has managed to bring good even from sin and death. This latter combination continually disrupts the project of the final community of love, but at the end we will see that it has in fact been interwoven into its fabric.

- Grace is God's response to the disaster of human sin, and the costly love of the Three, revealed in the Lord's passion and death, will be seen to have been worth its price. It was indeed "necessary that the Messiah should suffer these things and then enter into his glory" (Lk 24:26). And since Christ does not suffer alone, our own costly love will be seen to have played its part in forging the final glory of the race. Our sufferings benefited others: in our solidarity we made up for what was wanting in the body of humankind (cf. Col 1:24).

- We now often think that life is not worth the pain, but God judges that it is, and as creatures we try to accept this, but in blind faith. We will see that it was indeed true that "the sufferings of this present time are not worth comparing with the glory about to be revealed to us" (Rm 8:18). Malice and cruelty will reveal their bright side in the goodness they occasioned in others.
- What perhaps will amaze us most will be the revelation of the endless care on God's part to care for "enemies" and to bring them round. The Good Shepherd truly has searched for the lost sheep, and we may hope has brought them all safely home.
- We often say when faced with a tragic situation, "Why doesn't God do something about it?" But then we will recognize that ours is a compassionate God who has suffered with us, and has indeed done enough, especially through the Passion. We will see how God has wrestled with every evil and pain and brought surprising good from them. God will then wipe away every tear from our eyes (Rev 21:4), and we who now weep will laugh (Lk 6:21). And we will laugh not alone but with one another and also with the three divine Persons. We will see the truth of the remark made earlier that the human epic may be compared with a joke — the laughter comes at the end.

Our good Lord said: "You will see for yourself that every kind of thing will be well." There is a deed which the blessed Trinity will perform on the last day. Just as the blessed Trinity created all things from nothing, just so will the same blessed Trinity make everything well which is not well.[9]

This conviction is expressed well in the popular hymn "Lord, may you be blessed, for all is well." God will elevate the human story to a new level and merge it with the divine. There is a divine and human authorship of the *Complete History of Humankind!*

Joy

The Happy Twist

With Christianity, joy comes to the foreground of human living. In Luke's Gospel most of all, joy is linked with the presence of

---

9. Julian of Norwich *Showings*, p. 32.

Jesus. At the annunciation, the visitation and the birth of Jesus, joy is the central theme. And so through the Gospel. Jesus is Joyous News for all who can take it in. Joy filled the couple at Emmaus when they recognized him, and the Gospel closes with the disciples returning to Jerusalem "with great joy" (Lk 24:52). Joy is meant to be the mark of every Christian, because they are in the presence of God who is joy itself.

To catch the nature of the joy which we will experience in the world of God, let us turn for a moment to J. R. R Tolkien, the master of fairytale. He coined the word "eucatastrophe" to denote the sudden happy turn in a story which pierces us with a joy that brings tears.[10] It is a sudden glimpse of Truth. Our whole nature feels a sudden relief as if a major limb out of joint had suddenly snapped back. The resurrection is the greatest eucatastrophe and leads to joy. The consolation of the happy ending comes through a totally unexpected twist in the tale. The sudden joyous turn is a sudden and miraculous grace. It denies, in the face of much evidence, universal final defeat: the twist is Christ's incarnation and resurrection, the greatest and most complete eucatastrophe. This is the *evangelium*, the Good News. As Jesus promised his disciples: "You have pain now; but I will see you again, and your hearts will rejoice, and no one will take your joy from you" (Jn 16:22-24).

Joy will indeed be the serious business of heaven, as C. S. Lewis has said. God's joy will endlessly surprise. Great music such as Schiller's "Ode to Joy" in the final movement of Beethoven's *Ninth Symphony*, and Handel's "Alleluia Chorus" in the *Messiah*, gives a hint of this joy. Music itself will of course be prominent as an element of our joy. Given that tastes differ, no doubt each of us will hear the music that we find most appealing!

Each a Joyful Mystery

Each of us will experience joy and wonder in and about ourselves. We were a mystery to ourselves in this life: often we felt inadequate,

---

10. "Eucatastrophe" is coined from the Greek *eu* ("good") and *catastrophe* ("destruction"). See Tolkien's *Tree and Leaf* (1964), *On Fairy-Stories* (1947) and his letters (*The Letters of J. R. R. Tolkien*, Humphrey Carpenter, ed., Boston, Mass.: Mariner Books, 2000).

unworthy, ashamed. As someone said of a neighbor: "We're all mysteries of religion, and she's all the Sorrowful Mysteries in one!" It is a commonplace in Christian tradition to say that only by being a true friend to oneself can one be a good friend to others. At the End we will know fully who we really are and see our stories as essential ingredients in the cosmic adventure of humankind. There will be the never-ending wonder and joy in finding out that we are important. The New Testament notes that Christ is in us, "our hope of glory" (Col 1:27). A fundamental meaning of the word "glory" is "importance." The glory of a king meant that the king was important; if defeated in battle he became unimportant and his glory disappeared. The promise made to us is that there is "a glory about to be revealed in us" (Rm 8:18). We seemed to one another to be very ordinary in this life. But at the End we will enjoy "the freedom of the glory of the children of God" (Rm 8:21). Wonder and admiration for each other will be the order of the day, and that day will never end.

Summary

1. The divine project is to bring all humankind into the final community of love.
2. The world to come is all about relationships, and these will be perfected at the End. Only when the last person is finally gathered in will we see how all our stories fit together, and our individual and corporate glory will be revealed.
3. The three divine Persons will be revealed in their magnificence, and praise will ring out across the cosmos.
4. Joy is the serious business of heaven. Our joy will be complete (cf. Jn 16:20-24).

For Pondering

◊ Think of some experiences that you wish could last. Do you think that heaven could be like that?

Our Transfiguration

The Resurrection of the Body

About 50 AD, a one-time Pharisee and persecutor of Christians stood up in front of the Areopagus in Athens and proclaimed that a man, Jesus, had been resurrected. But "When they heard of the resurrection of the dead, some scoffed" (Acts 17:32).

James Joyce, too, scoffs at the notion of resurrection in a hilarious passage in *Ulysses*:

> The resurrection and the life. Once you are dead you are dead. That last day idea. Knocking them all up out of their graves. Come forth, Lazarus! And he came fifth and lost the job. Get up! Last day! Then every fellow mousing around for his liver and his lights and the rest of his traps. Find damn all of himself that morning. Pennyweight of powder in a skull.[11]

In contrast, we have one of the most exciting promises in the New Testament, which we noted before: "We will be like him, for we will see him as he is" (1 Jn 3:2). St. Paul dismissed certain questions about the nature of the resurrected body as foolishness (1 Cor 15:35) so what can we say about our physical transformation? It helps to recall that the context is the *koinonia*, that set of relationships in which the three divine Persons are the anchors. Within the three is Jesus, and it is because he is in solidarity with us, that we shall become like him.

Christian life means a state of friendship between Jesus and ourselves. Friends become alike, and when one of the partners is divine, the change in the other will be very deep indeed. In this life we "ought to walk just as he walked" (1 Jn 2:6): in the next life we will be brought further and will become what he is. The transfiguration of Jesus on the mountain (Mk 9:2-8) will be ours too. It was not a momentary show to dazzle the disciples but a hint of our destiny — glorious, radiant, spellbinding.

---

11. James Joyce, *Ulysses* (Oxford: Oxford University Press, 1993), p. 102.

Bodily Resurrection

In an older theology influenced by Greek thought, the superiority of soul/spirit over corruptible matter was presumed. Hence the resurrection of the body was seen as of minor importance, and the Church is still slow to adopt the Hebrew insight that human persons are constituted by an intimate bonding of body and soul such that neither can fully be without the other. The New Testament says simply "Christ is risen" — not a spiritualized Christ but the complete integrated Christ. His soul does not "escape" from matter to achieve its true destiny.

The doctrine of the assumption, 1950, states that the Mother of God is also in bodily glory. Vatican II places Mary not above but within the Church: she is the image and the first flowering of the Church as it is to be perfected in the world to come.[12] As she is, we will be. The Vatican in 1979, however, caution against presuming that we will be like Mary and her Son in bodily glory immediately after death.

Clearly there is more work to be done to liberate eschatological realities from the intra-worldly limits of space and time. Since there is no time in heaven, perhaps the "Last Day" for each of us is to be understood as the day we die. Let us say simply that as Jesus now is, so we will be. We will be fully integrated persons: we will be "revealed with Christ in glory" (Col 3:1), that is, in our risen bodies — immortal, incorruptible, agile, free, joyous, glorious. The "joy of our youth" will be restored to us: we will be freed from crippling illnesses of body, mind and heart. No more wheelchairs and Zimmer frames nor pain-relieving drugs! In the ecstasy of the transfigured body we will shine out as part of the "new creation" (Gal 6:15), our inner splendor no longer concealed. Through the incarnation and the paschal mystery there is in fact only one "body" now, the body of Christ, and it will be radiant with eternal glory.

Matter

God is always giving himself to us through matter. We do not have to evade creation to meet God at the End. We are part of God's history through the incarnation: his story and our stories interlink. In

---

12. See *Lumen gentium*, n. 63, n. 68.

the incarnation, God is given to us in Christ: he takes on matter, so matter is transformed. The Eucharist indicates the ongoing transformation of matter through the power of God and anticipates the ultimate transformation of all creation. St. Thomas Aquinas remarks that all creatures according to their mode naturally love God above all things in that they desire the fullness of life: all is made by God and seeks to return to God.

Karl Rahner has speculated that through death we enter into a new unlimited relationship with matter and share with Christ in the creation of the "new heavens and the new earth." Already we relate to matter endlessly: but matter and energy are convertible, since all matter came from energy. Matter has a dynamic face. When we are liberated from the limitations of space and time, we will relate to matter in a new and freer way. Science again holds that all material reality is interconnected. We may believe that after death we become open to all material being in its manifold forms.

Eternal Rest?

Why this emphasis until recently on "rest" as a dominant quality of the life to come? The desire for rest has a long history: "In toil you shall eat of the ground all the days of your life" (Gen 3:17). Endless labor was the lot of nomads and slaves in this life. So it was for the Jews in Egypt, in the desert and in Babylon. So for Christian slaves. Death then was liberation from a burdensome existence. Belief grew that the next life would be the opposite: it would be endless rest. Death and sleep were linked, as Jesus did in referring to Lazarus. Requiem Masses took their title from the notion of rest (Latin: *requies*).

All of this led to an image of eternal life as passive. But while the element of resting from toil will be present, God is Life, so those with him will be fully alive. There are no "dead" persons in the Christian vision of the life to come. "The glory of God is the human person fully alive" according to St. Irenaeus, the first systematic theologian, writing about 188 AD.

In Charge of Many Things

From the beginning, God is shown as energetic, and as engaging us in the task of the development of creation. Thus we are to "fill the earth and subdue it" (Gen 1:28). Whenever God decides to encounter his people, it is to commission them, to entrust them with tasks which will help his people. Thus Moses and the prophets, Mary and Jesus, Paul and the first disciples, are all given their mission, as is the Church itself. We may believe, then, that when we are fully with God, with gifts and talents perfected, we will be commissioned for new service to the people we have loved. They will still need our help, and as continuing members of the Network of Good People we will intercede and work for their well-being. Karl Rahner comments on Jesus using the image of being in the heart of the earth after his death: he suggests that we may be there with him, using our gifts to shape human history as it emerges. "I will put you in charge of many things!" (Mt 25:21, 23).

What Will We Do All Day?

Hugo Rahner's short but marvelous book, *Man at Play*, notes that work is linked to play when it is spontaneous and freely engaged in. God, he says, plays in creation.[13] Surely we will enjoy what God invites us to do, and just as God is happy, we too will be happy and playful. We will, as the lullaby puts it, have "the stars and moon to play with, the sun to run away with." All the good that is hinted at in this life will then be presented to us in its fullness. We love beauty:

> then all will be radiant in beauty, and we will be startled by it and contemplate its source, "beauty's self and beauty's giver."[14]

Here we admire artists who have gifts which we lack. But in heaven will we each be creative artists in our own right? Freed from space and time, surely we will admire and also participate in the unfolding of creation. To see creation from the outside as we do now is marvelous: to see it from the inside will be so much more

---

13. Hugo Rahner, *Man at Play* (London: Burns & Oates, 1972), pp. 11–25.
14. Gerard Manley Hopkins, "The Leaden Echo and the Golden Echo," *Poems and Prose*, ed. W. H. Gardner (London: Penguin, 1953), p. 54.

so. We will look in at the rich storehouse of nature in all its glory.
If it is true, for instance, that plants keep all colors except the one
they show, what will it be like to see a daffodil from the inside?
When we awaken after death, what breathtaking worlds will open
up to us? Will all aspects of present living be relativized? Will our
dramatic entry into a divine world of color and shape, beauty and
harmony, remind us of what human birthing hinted at? Will our
time-bound reality then be recognized as a short introduction to true
and vibrant existence with God? Will the agonizing and discordant
notes of human history then remind us of an orchestra warming up
in preparation for the great symphony we are about to enjoy? When
we are suddenly overwhelmed by light and the boundless dimensions
of reality, will we recall that here below we were like the prisoners
in Plato's cave (*Republic,* Book 7) who lived in darkness and a two-
dimensional world? When we meet God will we realize that all our
lives were spent in searching for "the one thing necessary"? Will the
pure desire to know and the limitless yearnings of the human heart
which exercised us in this life be seen as child-like attempts to reach
the Being, God, who now unfolds infinite love and wisdom to us?

Joy in Others

None of us gets relationships right all the time. My mother used
to feel this, but toward the end of her life she found the line of a
hymn which she quoted over and over: "All I ask of you is forever
to remember me as loving you." In the world to come, there will
be no awkward relationships: all of them will flow, endlessly. Surely
we will have time for ourselves, but also we will become incurable
romantics, relating with everyone, and each at their best. Endless
connections will be made and delighted in. We will see how others
have influenced us and we them, and how those we thought little of
have been vastly important, because with God there are no outsiders,
no one "surplus to requirements." The silent prayer and inner splendor of humble hearts will be seen to have helped us all. There will
be multiple fallings in love, and friendships will flower everywhere.
Ending his commentary on life everlasting, St. Thomas Aquinas says:

Finally, eternal life consists in the joyful companionship of all the blessed, a companionship which is full of delight. They will all love one another as themselves, and therefore will rejoice in one another's happiness as if it were their own.[15]

How will we relate to one another through our transfigured bodies? Bodily beauty will be revealed in its full glory. Will the transitory ecstasy of sexual fulfillment then be eternalized? Aquinas magisterially asserts that with the full actualization of our potentialities, all bodily delights will be ours because then they will be ordered and harmonious:

> Whatever is delightful will all be there superabundantly. Thus if we desire pleasure, there will be supreme and most perfect delight, in that its object will be God the sovereign good: "In your right hand are pleasures for evermore."[16]

Leonardo Boff puts things thus:

> At the end will be the festival of redeemed humankind. It will be the celestial dance of the freed, the banquet of sons and daughters in the homeland and household of the Trinity. In divinized creation we shall leap and sing, praise and love the Father, Son and Holy Spirit. And we shall be loved by them, praised by them, invited to dance and sing, sing and dance, dance and love, forever and forever. Amen.[17]

Summary

1. We will be like God, for we will see him as he is. Jesus' transfiguration gives a hint of our own.
2. God will engage our gifts in the task of the world's salvation: we will be "in charge of many things."
3. We will play, and we will explore God's creation from the inside.

For Pondering

◊ Can you imagine something of what your own transfiguration might mean?

---

15. Brev 2:785.
16. Ibid.
17. Leonardo Boff, *Trinity and Society* (London: Burns & Oates, 1988), p. 231.

The Completion of History

A Doubtful Future

Science forecasts that in less than five billion years the sun will burn up the earth: human life will have disappeared beforehand. What will be left? A silent and colorless cosmos, with no one to hear, no eye to admire? Cormac McCarthy's *The Road* pictures a devastated world and humanity at the edge of extinction. Is this how it will be? Or will the death of the universe be simply the end of one chapter and the opening of another in the unfolding drama of creation?

"Christ Will Come Again"

The Scriptures speak of a glorious appearance of Jesus which will bring a definitive close to the current chapter in human epic, as when St. Matthew speaks of the Son of Man "coming in his glory" (25:31). The Church looks for "the *glorious manifestation* of our Lord, Jesus Christ."[18] There is a spectrum of views around this event, which is not surprising, since we are grappling with the unparalleled mystery of God's decisive intervention in human affairs. As noted, the early Church was overwhelmed by the resurrection of Jesus — all the more are we out of our depth in speaking of the way in which God will bring the divine project to its completion.

Will the glorified Christ come back into our world from heaven, or will the Jesus event continue to unfold from within history as the high point of the evolutionary process? Jesus promised not to leave us but to be with us "to the end of the age" (Mt 28:20). From this latter perspective, when the *koinonia* is complete and divinized the full Christ, head and body, will be transparent to everyone in full glory, and so the *parousia* will emerge from within the womb of history rather than from outside.

Three converging terms are used in the New Testament to hint at our ultimate future: *parousia*, *pleroma* and *omega*.

---

18. *Dei Verbum*, n. 1, n. 4.

Parousia

This Greek term meaning "personal presence" was used when a ruler came to visit his people. The early Church longed for Jesus to be no longer hidden but to return visibly and in glory, so that the *koinonia* could celebrate its final victory. *Parousia* is a visible, tangible event, which suits our human need. Hence the New Testament closes with the Lord saying: "Surely I am coming soon," to which the response is: "Amen. Come, Lord Jesus" (Rev 22:20). The Eucharistic Prayers acclaim: "Christ has died. Christ is risen! *Christ will come again!*" *Parousia* then is understood as that moment in earth time when Christ closes human history. The *parousia* will vindicate Christ's triumph over evil and reveal the eternal glorious destiny of humankind.

Pleroma

This Greek term meaning "fullness" is often used by St. Paul in reference to the final completion of the Body of Christ, which is God's project underlying human history. Relationships will be in harmony. The cosmos will be filled with the divine presence.

Omega

Pierre Teilhard de Chardin focuses on the term *omega*, to provide an insight into the completion of human history. For him, *omega*, the last letter in the Greek alphabet, refers to Christ bringing all creation back to God who is the *alpha*, the first, the creator (see Rev 1:18). *Omega* will be the final moment of evolution. The task set us by God is to collaborate in the divinization of the Cosmic Christ, through the socialization of humankind.

De Chardin was fascinated by the continual increase in consciousness of matter as it develops in complexity. With the appearance of Christ, divine consciousness emerges. The divinization of humanity begins with Jesus and continues accordingly as human beings put on the mind and heart of Christ Jesus (cf. Phil 2:5). If all goes well, everyone will finally share the divine consciousness.

Christian Hope

In older views of eschatology, the second coming eclipsed the importance of the ongoing saving presence of Christ in the world. The *parousia* was reduced to an ultimate division of humankind into saved and damned. But in a Christo-centric theology, history now is *saving history*, rather than a catastrophe dragging to an inglorious end. The Lord is never absent from his friends.

Belief in the *parousia* is meant to transform our attitude to the present world. We are given ineradicable hope by its promise. It can give us courage to risk everything because the ultimate future is certain victory. "We wait in joyful hope for the coming of our Savior Jesus Christ." But we are not to wait passively. Part of the work of the *parousia* is ours: through our efforts to create community we advance the new world order established by Jesus.

Jesus' encounters with people were constructive. His miracles highlighted this and hinted at a future and better world. Jesus saw clearly what we are but also what we can become. He worked with the shortcomings of those who opposed him, rather than eliminating them. He transformed evil rather than wiped it away. We are to take our cue from him, and work with others to shape the possibilities of the world for good. As de Chardin says, we must try everything for Christ, we must love the world and give ourselves over passionately to its development. Influenced by de Chardin's breadth of thinking, *Gaudium et spes* challenges us to expand our hopes for the world till they match those of God.[19]

Thus, while the Absolute Future is pure gift — God's glorious communication of himself to us revealed in all its glory — it is not an event which will begin in the remote future! Even now Christ is at the center of history with those who are his friends. He is the destiny of the world and of the individual: he stands in solidarity with us now and forever. There is purpose and richness to every human life, and Christians carry a message of hope for the world. The participation by everyone in the final glory of things is a legitimate hope and aspiration.

A Transformed World

Rowan Williams remarks that our present ecological crisis has a great deal to do with our failure to think of the world as existing in

---

19. *Gaudium et spes*, n. 39.

relation to the mystery of God: instead we see it as a huge warehouse of stuff to be used for our convenience.

Until the current explosion of ecological concerns, St. Paul's concern for the cosmos found little echo in Christian thinking. How does the world relate to the mystery of God? Will earth disappear, or will a transformed cosmos always be home to us? Will we enter into a new relationship with that amazing stuff we call matter, which we now understand only a little but manipulate so tragically?

The opening chapter of Genesis proclaims that the cosmos is the work of God, who finds it good, not suspect or messy. St. Paul affirms his hope that creation will terminate not in dust but in glory and transfiguration. Creation will not be obliterated as no longer necessary. Instead it will be freed from bondage and decay and receive the liberty of the children of God. Now creation groans (Rm 8:21-22) and is disfigured, then it will be perfect and will reveal fully the glory of God. A new heaven and new earth will emerge (Rev 21:1ff) and God will be "all in all" (Eph 1:10). There will be a new creation (Is 65:17; Rev 21) — not a totally different world but a renovated one. The *Dictionary of Biblical Theology* states:

> The present form of the world will finally disappear ... in order that regenerated humanity may find its joy in *a universe completely renewed* ... The total sweep of Scripture invites the hope that a redeemed and freed creation will forever remain the world of God's children gathered together in Christ.[20]

The bishops at Vatican II expressed a new appreciation of this world so blessed by God and in which God is forever rooted due to the incarnation of the Son. Surely, they felt, this world cannot simply be consigned to the cosmic scrap heap. They say:

> We do not know when or how the universe *will be transformed*. But the form of this world, distorted by sin, is passing away, and God is preparing a new heaven and a new earth in which righteousness dwells, whose happiness will fill and surpass all the desires for peace arising in human hearts. Then death will have been conquered, the daughters and sons of God will be raised in Christ, and what was sown in weakness and dishonor will become incor-

---

20. *Dictionary of Biblical Theology*, under "World" and "Work."

ruptible; charity and its works will remain and all of creation, which God made for humanity, will be *set free from its bondage to decay.*[21]

We are not simply "souls" — we are spirit in matter. We must not try to escape from the world: we are rooted in it, children of the universe. The incarnation of Christ transforms our world and human activity plays its part in God's final shaping of the universe. In this view, nothing of good that we have achieved through our labors will be lost.

Balthasar offers the image of a disfigured bronze masterpiece which is recast in fire, only to emerge in unexpected splendor. Can we improve on this? It is a comfort for us who grieve at the defacing of our garden planet to know that just as God made all things simply by willing them to be, God can make all things new with his creating word. Aquinas says that the whole universe, created in love and sent forth by God, will be drawn back by love to God. And divine love is transformative.

Intimations of transformation are all around us: a beam of sunshine lighting up a dull autumn landscape; the break of dawn over dark mountains; the coming of spring; the turning on of a light in a beautiful room — there are innumerable hints of how life and color may emerge from cosmic darkness. Life on earth may well end in some five billion years, but this does not mean that the universe will become silent, dead and unaware. Rather we can believe that it will become vibrant with a transfigured humankind that has by God's grace transcended the boundaries of space, time and corruptibility.

Summary

1. Jesus saw clearly both what we are and what we can become.
2. Scripture invites us to hope in the complete renewal of the universe, as the home of transfigured humankind.
3. Our work makes an essential contribution to the development of creation. Nothing good that we have achieved will be lost.

---

21. *Lumen gentium,* n. 39.

For Pondering

◊ Do you look forward to meeting Christ openly? Would you wish to meet him sooner or later? Does it make you glad to think that nothing good will be lost?

"I am Making all Things New!"

Too Good to be True?

An Irish missionary in Zambia took a break from his labors one day and sat on the banks of the Zambesi. In the early afternoon he saw a boat coming from the far shore: it was hauled up below him and four men stepped out. Three of the men set off inland, so the missionary went down to chat to the man who had stayed behind. He was told that the other three had gone to the mission: they wanted to become Christians. "And you?" asked the missionary. "No" said the man, "your God is too good to be true. A god that becomes like us and gets killed by bad people and then rises again from death and forgives everyone and brings them with him to heaven — that's too good to be true!"

The divine project of our eternal joy seems indeed too good to be true, and my account of it may appear extravagant, but I believe it stands firmly on what has been revealed to us. In the past God has been presented as solitary, narcissistic, unmoved, dominant, an outsider to the created world. Our emphasis instead has been on a God who, as Elizabeth Johnson says, is relational, affiliated, connected, engaged, empowering, collegial, and also compassionate and suffering. Had I written *The Dummies' Guide to Eschatology*, key lines might have been: "We're going to be alive, happy, free forever!" "God gets around the problem of our sin!" "God wants to share everything with us!"

"God has a dream of human community that gets started in this life, and gets topped off in the next!" "We're all in this together, so play your part in shaping good relationships now!" "Too good to be true? Yes, but it happens. Good for God!"[22]

---

22. For an imaginative picture of what we stumble into after death, see C. S. Lewis, *The Last Battle* (London: Collins, 2008). The lion, Aslan, a Christ-figure, says to the children: "'Your father and mother and all of you are — as they used to call it in the Shadowlands — dead. The term is over: the holidays have begun. The dream is ended: this is the morning.'... All their life in this world ... had only been the cover and the title page:

The Demand

A perhaps surprising outcome of this book is the clear call to engage with God now in transforming our world, so to become fully alive ourselves, and enable others to be so too. The divine project of a transformed order of relationships — no longer slave or free, male or female, Jew or Greek (cf. Gal 3:28; Col 3:11) — demands *agape* love, even at the risk of death; this is the *koinonia* in process. The shock of bumping into God at the End will be eased by the awareness that in an undramatic way we bump into the divine in our neighbor and in creation. Wherever right relationships are promoted, God is present and *agape* love gains a new foothold. We are indeed unqualified architects, but fostering human community, we help to complete the divine Sagrada Familia (Holy Family) behind Gaudi's dream.

All Things New!

Since our argument throughout has been drawn from divine revelation, we may conclude with the closing words of the Book of Revelation. God has the last word on the outcome of divine involvement in human history. God is already making all things new, for in God nothing is old, all is young and new. "Christ has brought all newness in bringing himself" (St. Irenaeus). What is touched by the divine becomes new again, as the Gospels illustrate.

The "new Jerusalem" will be the gathering of all peoples in the completed *koinonia*. The city represents human community, life together rather than apart and individualistic. Person and community will be supremely fulfilled. God will dwell with us, and since it is the nature of all love to want to be eternal, we will grow in knowledge and love of the divine Persons endlessly.[23] There will be no more grief. Betrothal and parenting images hint at the depths of intimacy between God and ourselves. Relationships will be harmonious, justice will prevail, victory over evil and death will be complete.

---

now at last they were beginning Chapter One of the Great Story which no one on earth has read: which goes on forever: in which every chapter is better than the one before" (pp. 221–2).

23. See Ignace Lepp, *Death and Its Mysteries* (New York: MacMillan, 1968), pp. 183–91.

In the transfigured cosmos we will shine out like bright stars (Phil 2:15). We will be fully at home with God and one another, because the graced relationships which now carry us forward despite all odds will happily be complete.

Then I saw a new heaven and a new earth;

for the first heaven and the first earth had passed away,

and the sea was no more. And I saw the holy city, the new Jerusalem,

coming down out of heaven from God,

prepared as a bride adorned for her husband. And I heard a loud voice from the throne saying,

"See,

the home of God is among mortals.

He will dwell with them;

they will be his peoples,

and God himself will be with them;

he will wipe away every tear from their eyes.

Death will be no more;

mourning and crying and pain will be no more, for the first things have passed away."

And the one who was seated on the throne said,

"See, I am making all things new." Then he said to me,

"It is done!

I am the Alpha

and the Omega, the beginning and the end.

To the thirsty I will give water as a gift

from the spring of the water of life. Those who conquer

will inherit these things, and I will be their God

and they will be my children." (Rev 21:1-7)

Summary

1. Christian hope is based on the firm belief that God through Christ will achieve the divine dream of bringing all of us, and the cosmos, to glory.
2. We are in solidarity with the risen Lord of history. Our task is to pray and labor in harmony with God so that the divine intention may be achieved.
3. At the End, Christ the Sower and we the reapers will sit and rejoice together because the harvest is complete (cf. Jn 4:36).

For Pondering

◊ Now that you have completed the book, have you a greater hope than before that God "will make all things well" and some sense of how God will bring this about?

Acknowledgments

Thanks firstly to my students at Milltown Institute, Dublin, and elsewhere, whose queries and comments provoked development in my own thinking. There is nothing so likely to send one back to the drawing board as the incredulous remark, "You don't *believe* that, do you?" Next, thanks to those who made constructive criticisms at various stages: Brendan Duddy SJ, Patrick Gallagher, Christine Gilsen and Eileen Houlahan CHF. Special thanks to Phyllis Brady and Anne Lyons PBVM, both of whom also proofread the text. I am grateful to my brother and my nephews whose humanist and scientific perspectives enlarged my thinking. On the practical level, thanks to Agata Dworzynska for numerous draft printings, and to Donna Doherty and Julie Steenson of Veritas who encouraged the project and brought it to completion.

Over the year of writing, a good friend was journeying toward death and beyond. Her path, which led through bewilderment, fear and suffering, impacted deeply on those close to her. For me, the harshness of her losing battle with cancer challenged abstract ideas and demanded an honest response. One of the themes of the book is that God works indefatigably in suffering to bring good from it. Good has come from my friend's dark pain and made these pages more real and true to life.

Since this book is for the general reader and is intended to be user-friendly, references have been kept to a minimum. The *New Revised Standard Bible*, 1989, has been used, with its inclusive language. Reference works frequently consulted include The *New Jerome Biblical Commentary* (1989), Xavier Leon-Dufour's *Dictionary of Biblical Theology* (MD, Word Among Us Press, 1988 edition) and the *Catechism of the Catholic Church* (Dublin: Veritas, 1992, abbreviated as *CCC*). Authors to whom I am deeply indebted include Hans Urs von Balthasar (1905–88), Teilhard de Chardin (1881–1955), John Hyde (1909–81), Elizabeth A. Johnson (1941–), C. S. Lewis (1898–1963), Bernard Lonergan (1904–84), Karl Rahner (1904–84) and Joseph Ratzinger (1927–).